SURPRISE

SURPRISe

Embrace the Unpredictable AND Engineer the Unexpected

TANIA LUNA
and
LEEANN RENNINGER, PhD

A PERIGEE BOOK

A PERIGEE BOOK
Published by the Penguin Group
Penguin Group (USA) LLC
375 Hudson Street, New York, New York 10014

USA • Canada • UK • Ireland • Australia • New Zealand • India • South Africa • China

penguin.com

A Penguin Random House Company

Library of Congress Cataloging-in-Publication Data

Luna, Tania.
Surprise : embrace the unpredictable, engineer the unexpected / by Tania Luna and
LeeAnn Renninger, PhD.
pages   cm
ISBN 978-0-399-16982-3 (hardback)
1. Surprise.   2. Emotions.   3. Adaptability (Psychology)   I. Renninger, LeeAnn.   II. Title.
BF575.S8L86   2015
152.4—dc23   2014043668

First edition: April 2015

PRINTED IN THE UNITED STATES OF AMERICA

10   9   8   7   6   5   4   3   2   1

Text design by Kristin del Rosario
Illustrations on pages xxiv, 23, 38, 70, 90, 98, and 168 copyright © by Jason B. Forest
Photo on page 6 copyright © by Steven Goldin
Photos on pages 8 and 195 copyright © by Tania Luna

To our husbands,
Brian and Dirk,
who are always surprising us.

··· CONTENTS ···

PART IV: EVERYDAY SURPRISE

Our Story

Hello, dear reader. We've only just met, but there are a few predictions we can already make about you. Your life is wrapped in uncertainties and complexities (even the things that seem simple rarely ever are). You find these spots of mystery and confusion frustrating. But they also intrigue you. Sometimes they even inspire you. You wish for fewer surprises in your life, and sometimes—when your calendar is packed with meetings that you can't seem to remember even as they're happening—you wish for more surprise. More wonder, more vibrancy, more adventure. We know how you feel because we've been there. Our personal stories of surprise have shaped our lives and led us to write this very book.

THE DARK DOOR: TANIA'S STORY

I place two fingers on my neck. It feels like a tiny creature is pounding against my carotid artery with its fists. Thud. Thud.

Thud. By now, it's a familiar sensation, but it still makes me giggle so uncontrollably that I have to hold my breath. I'm all grown up. Yet I feel as much delight in this moment as I did curled up in the bottom of some friend's closet during a game of hide and seek. The phone booth I'm standing in is snug and caked in gum. It smells like beer. But it's a good hiding spot. I'll be able to see them through the gap in the metal, but they won't be able to tell I'm watching. Besides, it's a bustling city street near Grand Central, so I am practically invisible. Someone walks past me. I grab the phone and press it to my ear. It's sticky. I regret it immediately. The pounding in my neck grows more insistent. I have to press my hand over my mouth to keep from bursting into laughter. The stranger keeps walking. False alarm. I exhale and permit a stray giggle to escape. I love my job.

Sometimes it's a little awkward explaining what I do for a living. I find it especially challenging at parties of the loud-music and small-talk variety.

"So what do you do?"

"I specialize in surprise."

"What did you say?"

"I surprise people!"

"You *what*?"

"Surprise!!!"

At this point, they either develop a sudden urge to go "check on something" or everything screeches to a halt and, to my deep discomfort, I become the center of attention. A blockade of eager faces piles up around me, expecting to be amused and delighted by my career choice. They say things like, "You must have so much fun!" And, "What was the best surprise you ever did?" I don't want to let them down, so I handpick the bits and pieces that make for good storytelling and reality television. But all the while, what I really want to do is turn down the music, invite them to pull up a cushy chair, and tell the story of the biggest surprise of all. It isn't silly or sensational. It doesn't make for good small talk. But it is the reason that I am writing this book: Embracing surprise changed my life.

I check the time and peer through the gap in the phone booth again. Waiting is the hardest part, but I savor the anticipation. Any minute now, the corner I'm watching will fill with anxious and excited faces—clients who have asked us to take them on a surprise. You'd think I'd be the calm one since I know the plan, but even after six years of plotting surprises, calm *is not a word that surfaces often in my vocabulary. I have a plan, yes, but things can change in an instant. I have to be ready to meet the swerving, swirling unpredictability of life head-on. I realize that I'm looking forward to something unexpected happening, and it makes me grin.*

I haven't always been this way. If you rewound to my child-hood you'd see a little girl who hated surprise so much that she forbade her family from getting her unexpected gifts for her birthday. (All presents had to be approved at least one week in advance.) As time went on, her surprise aversion only grew stronger and more sophisticated. By the time she was in high school, her computer brimmed with spreadsheets that outlined her life plans (in one-month, six-month, one-year, five-year, and ten-year increments). She even tracked the emotions she experienced and planned to experience in her relationships. The woman crouching in this sticky, boozy phone booth still feels a *thud thud thud* in her neck when giving up control, but she accepts it now. Most days, she even relishes it.

At last, they reach the corner. I recognize them just by their facial expressions. Some are giggling and poking each other like kids. Some clutch one another's arms. Others look borderline angry. I've come to know all these reactions to surprise as intimately as the excited pounding in my own chest. I grab my cell phone, type "cross the street," and push the "send" button. The text message flies across the street and all their phones buzz at once. As soon as they've followed my instructions, I type: "Good. Now get on the next train that arrives. You'll know when to get off." I know they've gotten the message because they turn in circles, trying to figure out how I can see them. My phone vibrates.

"Just get on?!?!?"

"Yes."

They don't know it yet, but they aren't just getting on the subway. They're walking into a living metaphor for our perpetually changing and surprising world. And it's not just a fun way to spend a Tuesday afternoon. It's training in the skills that separate people and organizations that thrive in this new world from the ones that can't stomach its volatility. Skills that most of us never developed because we were raised to believe in a world that's predictable and under our control. These skills distinguish the most successful businesses from the forgettable ones, fulfilling relationships from stale ones, and individuals who are passionate explorers from those who feel stuck and lost. They are the skills that turn our work and our lives into meaningful adventures. And they are the skills that have transformed me from an anxious, emotionally numb control freak into a jumble of joy inside a phone booth.

From Spreadsheets to Surprise

My sister, Kat, and I started the business that would become Surprise Industries with a question: "What if people could sign up for an unusual activity (anything from unicycling to ice sculpting) but have no idea what they'd be doing until they got there?" The experiment appealed to Kat, who loves collecting new experiences. And it appealed to me because I love surprising others (even though I hated being surprised myself). After that conversation, I stayed up all night crafting a business plan and, of course, lots of spreadsheets. I chuckled at the thought that I'd never want to be my own client, but I expected to have fun from the safety of the driver's seat.

As the business picked up steam, my illusions of control and predictability crumbled. I realized that I wasn't just out of the driver's seat—I wasn't even in the car. Most days I found myself on a rickety boat in the middle of an ocean with no map to guide me to land. I spent a lot of time doing the psychological equivalent of kicking and screaming. Okay, sometimes it was literal kicking and screaming. How would we find new clients? Who would be willing to sell us liability insurance? What was the best way to price our services? Nobody could give me the answers because nobody had ever tried to sell surprise. My morning routine began with "I don't want to get up," followed by doors slamming behind me all over the apartment. (For some reason, we have a lot of doors.) I didn't want to accept a world I couldn't organize into a spreadsheet. And yet, there it was—rising, falling, and swirling all around me.

Somehow I managed to come up for air long enough to realize that something special was happening in the midst of the entrepreneurial chaos. Our clients were transforming in strange and wonderful ways. They went into their surprise adventures hesitant but came out with a connection and vibrancy I had never experienced. I caught myself thinking, "I want that."

In the meanwhile, as though launching a company weren't confusing enough, I stumbled into a relationship with (my now husband) Brian. All my attempts at spreadsheeting my feelings or even plans for the weekend were rebuffed. Brian said things like "let go" and "just feel," which for me was the equivalent of telling a star-nosed mole to "just see." How could I let myself feel something that I couldn't package neatly into a sentence? How could I let go with no net to catch me?

Falling in love was both horrifying and magnificent. Before I knew what was happening, my business and relationship transformed my world from safe and predictable to perpetually surprising. I used to picture two giant doors looming over me. One door opened into a well-lit room. The other opened into infinite darkness. Walking through the first door meant giving up on my business, getting a "real" job, and slowing down my relationship. Entering the Dark Door meant giving Surprise Industries, Brian, and maybe even all my dreams everything I had. I stood before those imaginary doors for a long time until I finally stepped into the darkness.

The most startling aspect of my surprising new existence was the emotions. Feelings like wonder, fury, delight, sorrow, awe, hope, and joy filled me with an intensity I hadn't felt since my early childhood. I had learned to protect myself from negative emotions, but in doing so, I snuffed the good ones out. By keeping out the bad surprises, I stopped letting in the good ones.

In 2010, around the time that this realization really kicked in, I met the coauthor of this book, my beloved friend and colleague, LeeAnn Renninger. While I was observing surprise "in the field," LeeAnn was studying surprise in the laboratory. Aside from her work as a research psychologist, she is also the founder of LifeLabs New York, a training center for the work and life skills that few of us pick up in school: asking good questions, giving feedback, collaboration, resilience, and much, much more. She was engineering surprise to help companies better engage and train their employees. Best of all, she and I (with no knowledge of one another's existence) became obsessed with what we independently called Surprisology: the science of surprise.

We met for the first time at a café in Brooklyn. Two bubble teas later, we had a stack of ideas so thick they jammed our filing cabinets. It became clear that our goal was (and still is) to help individuals and companies embrace and engineer surprise so everyone could access the transformation we've seen in our clients and in ourselves. By the time our meeting ended we knew Surprise Industries and LifeLabs New York had to join forces. The idea for this book came out of that same momentous meet up.

ONLY BORING KIDS GET BORED: LEEANN'S STORY

It's safe to say that Tania and I are both infatuated with surprise, but we realized early on that surprise has played very different roles in our lives. Tania's challenge has been to embrace the surprises in her path. But I think for me, the worst thing in the world is not having *enough* surprise—that state of living but not feeling alive. And so, one of my missions has been to turn the volume up on life when it feels like I'm not getting enough out of it. It began when I was twelve years old.

My parents started a family project that was incredibly exciting to them. They decided to design and build a new house for us from the ground up. For me, as a preteen, this was exciting for exactly two weeks. But after those two weeks were up, I was still required to accompany my parents on every site visit. While all my friends were out playing, I would wander about the skeleton of our new house or sit off to the side and stare as the construction workers carried planks and buckets this way and that way. Despite my poor parents' attempts at keeping me entertained, for hours on end I was intensely, uncontrollably bored. One day, it occurred to me that I was suffering the worst fate in the world. No kid should be forced to join her family in a house-building project, I decided. Didn't they realize that I was far too interesting to waste my time on such things?

I had always been a good, obedient kid, but on that day, I was unstoppable. I felt that something had to be done to let the world know about the injustices in my life. And so, that night, when the construction site grew dark, I sneaked up to where the workers had just installed fresh blue insulation—my father's pride and joy. He always said we had to be careful with it because the slightest dent could let air in through the walls. I grabbed a screwdriver, pressed it into the insulation, and carved in the worst, most insulting word I could imagine. I wrote huge, angry letters followed by three very intentional exclamation marks:

BORING!!!

As in: This is boring. Y'all are boring. This house is boring. I'm above it all. Take that!

The next day at school, I realized that my huge BORING proclamation wasn't very nice. It wasn't my parents' fault that I was bored! They were always showing us new things and even traveling around the United States with us so that we could discover new places. By building the house, they hoped we would all have a new adventure together as a family. Instead of being grateful, I had become a vandal. I couldn't concentrate in class, eat lunch, or talk to my friends—all I could think about was how quickly I could get to the construction site and somehow replace the insulation I ruined with my impromptu etching. After school I sprinted to the house so hard that my throat burned and my heart pounded in my head. When I finally reached the site, I froze in my tracks. To my great surprise, someone had replied to my note. Using a Sharpie marker, someone had added four simple words to the front and back of my message:

Only BORING!!! Kids Get Bored!

The fear I had been carrying all day turned into outrage. "What?! How dare someone say this! This place is boring, not me! I am not a boring kid!" I thought, staring back at that wall defiantly. But then I thought, "Or am I?"

My dad—whose handwriting I was pretty sure I recognized—didn't say anything about the words. The next day, the construction workers placed drywall over them. The words were left right at the entryway to our house so that I had to walk through them every single day when I came home. They became a part of the house, and they became a part of me.

From then on I made it my mission to never be bored again. I quickly learned that the ultimate boredom antidote is surprise. I started entering the construction site with fresh eyes, searching for anything unusual and unexpected in the place I thought I knew better than the alphabet. I mixed odd things like cement with mud and mulch to see what would happen. I sat by the road for hours with my experiments. Noticing my newfound curiosity, my mother bought me a microscope and, along with the construction workers, I examined everything I found. Concrete, insulation, spit, and peanut butter sandwiches all got my attention. When I wasn't peering into the microscope, I was making obstacle courses and timing my progress. In school, I filled myself with wonder like helium in a balloon. I searched for surprise everywhere, even managing to notice interesting things about Mrs. Mertz—formerly the world's most boring homeroom teacher. Instead of sitting around and waiting for something interesting to happen, I became an engineer of the unexpected. My life turned into a quest for surprise.

The quest continued. In college I studied experimental psychology and left my hometown in Pennsylvania to do graduate research in Hawaii, the United Kingdom, and at the University of Vienna in Austria. There, just when I needed it most, I had another run-in with surprise.

Finding Authentic Happiness in Unexpected Places

With the help of a computer program that tracks facial expressions, I had spent several weeks examining footage of participants describing their happiest memories. It may sound like an interesting topic, but by that point, in my mind, it was nothing more than data. An all-consuming curiosity had brought me to this lab, but the allure had faded (or maybe it was just obstructed by the growing piles of data I had to enter and papers I had to grade). One day, I muted the recordings of people's happy stories so that I could concentrate on the program's analysis. My eyes burned, and my mind felt numb. Without realizing it, I had let myself get bored again.

Then, something peculiar about the output caught my attention. It had nothing to do with my research, but I found myself drawn to it anyway. Most participants exhibited a combination of facial muscle micro-movements categorized as contentment or satisfaction (that nice, soft feeling we get when inhaling a fresh breeze or tasting a perfectly ripened strawberry), but every once in a while a spike in the data told me that participants felt an emotion called *authentic happiness.* As far as emotions go, authentic happiness is the real deal. It's not a politely synthesized smile or a reaction to a good cup of coffee. It's that all-encompassing sense of joy that feels like butterflies and champagne bubbles in your chest. It makes your eyes crinkly and your cheeks hurt from smiling. True, giddy, dancing-in-the-rain kind of happiness. Most participants didn't experience it, but a few did. How come?

I turned up the volume and scoured the footage to see if a pattern existed. Sure enough, it did. The happiest participants shared memories that contained an element of surprise. They weren't necessarily fairytale proposals or lottery victories. Many of the surprises weren't even altogether pleasant. One woman described having to hobble down the aisle on her wedding day with a broken high heel. Her eyes sparkled and her cheeks flushed as she recalled how her friends and family giggled, laughed, and finally burst into applause when she made it all the way down to her groom. Not exactly something you'd plan into the perfect wedding, but it turns out that it's not the perfectly planned and controlled moments that make us the happiest. It's the surprising ones.

There it was again: a reminder that surprise can make a big difference in the way we experience the world. *We feel most comfortable when things are certain, but we feel most alive when they're not.* I didn't want to waste another minute of my life not feeling alive.

A few years later, this discovery and the memory of the words carved into my childhood home inspired me to launch my company, LifeLabs New York. Eventually, I decided to design a workshop around the science of surprise and immediately went online to buy the domain name Surprisology.com. To my surprise (and dismay), someone already owned it. It was a blog belonging to Surprise Industries, a company specializing in . . . wait a minute . . . surprise?! In one of those reality-is-stranger-than-fiction scenarios, soon after I came across Surprise Industries, someone from the company called me to see if I wanted to collaborate. Um . . . yes!

When Tania and I first met, we placed our life stories side by side and saw something that has forever changed the way we look at our work, our relationships, and the world around us. Tania has learned to savor surprise by embracing the unpredictability in her life. This transformation lets her take bolder risks and follow her passion even though the road to its door is paved with the unknown. But embracing the unpredictable is only half the story. What I've had to learn is how to systematically engineer the unexpected—how to use surprise to create limitless access to that feeling of aliveness that I hold so dear. Best of all, these seemingly vast changes in our lives were extraordinarily simple. We didn't have to meditate every morning, drink green juices, go to therapy, take medication, or recite affirmations while looking in the mirror. All we had to do was understand how surprise works and how to use it as a tool.

Today, Surprise Industries still takes people on surprise adventures. And at LifeLabs New York, we use the science of surprise to make learning fun and sticky. We help companies reduce negative surprises and weave in more delightful ones. Tania and I hold workshops to spread awareness about the power of surprise, and we conduct research in surprise psychology. Countless times now, we've seen that understanding surprise sparks creativity, helps ideas spread, decreases anxiety, ends conflict, and makes our lives and work richer and more meaningful. The very word *surprise* has become a shortcut for us. Our aim is to give that shortcut to you.

UP AHEAD: BY TANIA AND LEEANN

What you are about to read is not exactly a self-help book. We aren't going to present six secret steps to wealth and happiness or the five pillars of success. Instead, we'll share our lens with you: the world, as we've come to know it, from the perspective of surprise. Though we are both psychologists, researchers, educators, and entrepreneurs, first and foremost we are Surprisologists. This book is an ode to surprise and an invitation to you, the reader, to see the world through the eyes of a Surprisologist too.

You are about to discover how to make your work and life even more extraordinary. You'll learn how surprise plays a major role in your work, relationships, and day-to-day life. You will develop new skills that are vital in our modern world. You'll understand how to better embrace the unpredictable. And you will become an agent of surprise with even more power than you already have to engineer the unexpected. You'll find it easier to follow your passion, cultivate your relationships, and lead a more invigorating existence. You'll break through the noise and make a deeper impact on others. If all this sounds too good to be true . . . don't be a skeptic, man.

In the next two chapters, we'll give you a micro and macro view of surprise, exploring how it works in your brain and in your world. Next, you'll learn how to embrace surprise so that it never looms as a threat over the horizon or acts as an obstacle in your path. After that you'll get even better at engineering surprise for others. And last but not least, you will understand how to skillfully infuse surprise into your relationships and everyday life for more vibrancy and fulfillment. Along the way, you'll learn fascinating research and meet inspiring individuals who embrace and engineer surprise. Whether our stories take you to Namibia or New York, to classrooms or prisons, you will find nuggets of insight that you can apply to all aspects of your life. We think the power and simplicity of what you are about to learn will surprise you.

PART ONE

Understand SURPRISE

*Our brightest blazes of gladness are
commonly kindled by unexpected sparks.*
—SAMUEL JOHNSON

Let's begin with a surprise quiz. Don't worry; you've had your
whole life to prepare.

1. What is surprise?
   A. *An emotion*
   B. *A mental state*

2. Where do you feel surprise in your body?
   A. *Stomach*
   B. *Chest*
   C. *Face*

3. How do you look when you are surprised?
   A. *Bulging eyes*

B. *Gaping mouth*

C. *A & B*

D. *None of these*

4. How often do you feel surprise?

A. *Rarely*

B. *Occasionally*

C. *Often*

D. *Every day*

Turn this book upside down to get the right answers.

Just kidding. There are no right answers. When we ask these questions in our workshops and during our keynotes, the answers are so varied you'd think we were all a different species. Scientists still debate over what surprise is, where it happens in the body, and even how the facial expression of surprise really looks.

Given that surprise exists in every culture, you'd think we'd have it figured out by now.[1] But surprise remains elusive and widely misunderstood. Some psychologists call it an emotion. Others argue that it's a cognitive state.[2] Among the biggest misconceptions about surprise is that it happens rarely. The truth is, we humans are surprised all the time. And you are about to get really good at spotting when it happens in your brain and in your world.

Surprise in the Brain

Imagine you're perched on a boulder about 200,000 years ago, cradling a handful of succulent berries. Beside you sits your pal, Caveman Bill. Together you are savoring this luscious treat, thinking of nothing but the juicy sweetness at your lips, when all of a sudden out leaps a drooling, snarling saber-tooth. What do you do?

If you have the capacity to feel surprise, you freeze with the berries still half-chewed in your mouth and hyper-focus. In less than a second, your brain takes note of the fangs, the claws, and the not-so-friendly body language. It makes a value judgment (*This is bad.*). It pulls in information from the environment (where to run and where to hide). Next, your other reflexes kick in, and you're running faster than an Olympic sprinter (only the Olympics don't exist yet). If this experience doesn't kill you, it makes you smarter. You probably share your story with your cave-dwelling friends, helping them get smarter too.

Now let's take a look at what happened to Caveman Bill. Bill didn't inherit the genes that enabled him to be surprised, so his response to the saber-tooth was different. Namely, he just stood there, chewing his berries. Thanks to your reaction, you got away and went on to pass your surprise genes to your offspring, and poor Caveman Bill went on to become prehistoric brunch.

With the help of surprise, our ancestors also spotted chances to eat, drink, and mate. Surprise protected them from danger and pointed them toward opportunity. Today, feeling surprise is rarely a matter of survival, but our bodies are still hardwired to experience it with the same intensity. That explains why surprise plays a major role in our everyday lives (even if we don't notice it happening).

In this chapter, we delve deep into the brain to explore what surprise really is and how it affects our behavior. When possible, we draw from existing terms and theories or integrate theories proposed by various psychologists, neuroscientists, and behavioral economists. But surprise has gotten so little attention from the scientific community that in some cases we had to start from scratch and devise new ways to explain what surprise is and how it works.

At least one thing most scientists do agree on is that our brains (and the brains of most living things) are prediction machines—constantly sifting apart the expected and the unexpected. Whenever we *aren't* surprised, it's because we've managed to predict what would happen in the next instant with relative accuracy. We say "relative" accuracy because, in our most spookily psychic moments, we rarely predict every single feature of the environment. But so long as what happens is very close to what we thought would happen, our brains sit back peacefully with an "I told you so" kind of smirk. When we detect something we *didn't* predict, our brains get all riled up and jump into action.

THE SURPRISE SEQUENCE

Surprise is an event or observation that is either unexpected (*I didn't see that coming!*) or misexpected (*That's not what I thought was going to happen.*). In either case, it is a strong neural response that shouts, "You were wrong!" Regardless of whether the surprise is neutral (*I didn't know hippo milk was pink!*), pleasant (*I just won $500!*), or unpleasant (*I just got a bill for $500!*), all surprises trigger the same prehistoric sequence in our modern brains.

Most researchers have studied only one aspect of this sequence, so we've pulled together various findings into one overarching framework for understanding surprise. We call it the Surprise Sequence. When we are surprised we freeze, try to find an explanation, shift our perspective, and share our experience. Let's probe each layer of this sequence further.

Surprise Sequence Part One: Freeze

We lovingly refer to the facial expression illustrated on the next page as the Duh Face. It isn't the wide eyes and gaping mouth we associate with surprise but the fraction of a second in which our faces look completely devoid of self-awareness. Curiously, most of us assume our eyes and mouths open wide when we're surprised, but research reveals that few of us take on this stereotypical expression.[1]

When we first started surprising people at Surprise Industries, we anticipated the big, bold facial expressions of reality TV surprises. We armed ourselves with cameras to capture the exciting reactions. To our dismay our photo subjects looked very little like *Extreme Makeover: Home Edition* winners and very much like deer in the headlights. What we didn't realize was that the expression we associate with surprise is often exaggerated for the audience. This macro expression *communicates* to others that we are surprised, but the Duh Face is the truest expression of *feeling* surprise. This goofy, beautifully genuine expression is a sign of the first phase of the Surprise Sequence.

Surprise elicits a spike in the brain wave called the P300, which hijacks our cognitive resources and pulls our attention onto the object of surprise.[2] We've dubbed this phenomenon the *Freeze Phase*. As the psychologist Silvan Tomkins puts it, the Freeze Phase "is similar in design and function to that of a radio or television network which enables special announcements to interrupt any ongoing program."[3] To test the Freeze Phase, say something surprising while your friends are eating. Did their forks stop in midair? Did their mouths stop chewing and hang open?

The End

Did your P300 get riled up when you read "The End"? If you slowed down to focus on these unexpected words, you've just experienced the Freeze Phase. The interesting thing about this sensation is that it is involuntary. We don't have to force ourselves to pay attention. When we're surprised, we forget everything in the world and can't help but plug into the moment.

Surprise Sequence Part Two: Find

The Freeze Phase lasts for just an instant. After surprise stops us in our tracks and wins our attention, our brains suck in and analyze information at an incredible speed. This search for answers happens so quickly that we're usually not even aware of it. Look at the sequence of facial expressions in the images below.

In an experiment, we asked participants to watch a video with a surprising twist.[4] This is one of the reactions we captured on video. Recognize the first expression? It's our beloved Duh Face. But in just a fraction of a second, the woman shifts into other expressions: first overtly communicating surprise, then fear, and finally amusement—all within one second. What happened in her brain between the first and last image? We call it the *Find Phase*. Between the Duh Face and the emotional reaction, her mind was able to sort through a broad range of thoughts and questions and come to a conclusion about what she just witnessed.

The speed of the Find Phase is one of the reasons the Duh Face is tough to recognize. Almost immediately after we freeze in our tracks, we come to some conclusion about the surprise and reveal a follow-up emotion like fear, sadness, anger, or joy. But the Find Phase doesn't always stop there. As long as something unknown lingers in the situation, our minds generate more questions and form more hypotheses. Pick up any newspaper to catch this phenomenon in action. Archival research shows that after a surprising event like a plane crash or natural disaster, newspapers print more and more explanations over time.[5]

Do a quick search for surprise homecoming videos online, and you'll notice that after the initial shrieks, sobs, and embraces, surprised individuals interrogate the surprise plotters. "How did you get here?" "Does anyone else know?" "Are you staying for good?" Pleasant surprises we can't resolve (like finding an anonymous love letter) can stay with us for a lifetime—sparking a rush of excitement every time we come across them in our memories. Similarly, unpleasant surprises (like unexpected breakups) leave behind an endless stream of questions, making "moving on" much tougher than it would have been had we been expecting the event. Whether the surprise is wonderful or terrible, only after we have answers to the majority of our questions can we stop obsessing and consider the case closed.

Surprise Sequence Part Three: Shift

The intensity and duration of the Freeze and Find Phases of the Surprise Sequence depend on our degree of surprise. And our degree of surprise depends on our degree of schema discrepancy. A schema (plural: schemata) is an individual's framework for understanding something. For example, most of us have a cat schema: a compilation of ideas about how cats look, move, feel, and sound. If you encounter a cat that barks, you will experience a schema discrepancy (aka surprise). The only ways to get past the surprise are to pretend you never experienced it (*What barking cat?*), come up with a reasonable explanation (*That's just a dog that looks like a cat.*), or shift your schema (*I guess some cats bark some of the time.*). The point at which a change takes place in a schema is the *Shift Phase.*

Legendary psychologist Jean Piaget was fascinated by the role of surprise in our intellectual development. (We like to think of him as the Godfather of Surprisology.) He pointed out that children have incredibly flexible schemata. Their beliefs constantly shift and stretch to accommodate all they discover about life. Just watch kids explore a new environment. You'll see the Shift Phase in action. They gasp, they stare, they touch, they dig, they sniff. All the while their flexible little brains adjust and expand their understanding of the world. Each new surprise creates a fuller, richer tapestry of reality.

As we grow older and more experienced, our schemata get rigid. We resist learning new things and changing our perspectives. Surprise still freezes us involuntarily and pushes us to find an explanation, but the Shift Phase of the Surprise Sequence requires more effort. It can be so uncomfortable that we avoid new information and opinions.

Because of this resistance to updating our schemata, not every surprise creates an obvious shift. We often manage to explain surprise away. If you are a Democrat and believe that Republicans are closed-minded, you may be surprised when you meet a Republican who doesn't fit this stereotype. But instead of shifting your opinion about Republicans in general, you can protect your initial stance by saying something like, "This Republican is different from all the others" or "He's just telling me what I want to hear."

In addition to our stubborn schema maintenance, most of us also have a confirmation bias: a tendency to seek information that confirms our views and ignore information that challenges them. So if you're a Republican who believes Democrats are naive and misguided, you'll read articles and watch shows that paint Democrats in a negative light while staying clear of any evidence to the contrary. Through this ongoing, unconscious process, we protect and fortify our schemata. In other words, we keep the surprise out.

The Shift Phase isn't always immediate or obvious, but even when no change is visible on the surface, *shift happens*. When people change their minds it looks sudden, but it is usually the result of many surprises (many tiny shifts) accumulating over time—like grains of sand falling on a sand pile with no apparent effect until just one grain causes the entire pile to topple.

And when our schemata *do* shift, it's almost always as a result of surprise. This shift can happen to a specific opinion (*I didn't realize pit bulls were friendly!*), but it can also be a general shift in our mind-sets. Consider a study conducted by psychologist Norbert Schwarz.[6] Sneaky Schwarz hid coins in university copying machines, then interviewed students who discovered the surprise and students who did not. People who found a coin felt significantly happier and more satisfied with life than those who didn't find one. Thanks to the surprise, the students' views on the quality of their entire lives shifted. And here's the best part: The value of this happiness-producing coin was the German equivalent of a dime. It doesn't take a lot to buy happiness if you've got surprise on your side. Unfortunately, the same can be said about the power of negative surprises. Anyone who's ever spilled coffee on white pants knows that it also doesn't take a lot to ruin a perfectly good day. Surprise of all varieties is a force of change.

Surprise Sequence Part Four: Share

Whether a surprise is negative or positive, it is exhausting for our brains. Just think of all that freezing, finding, and schema shifting (or defending) we have to do. It's such tough work that surprise creates a cognitive burden.[7] We humans relieve this burden by sharing it with others. In other words, when we're surprised, we talk about it. Talking also helps us make sense of our experiences and forge a stronger connection with others. This process is the final stage of the Surprise Sequence: the *Share Phase*.

We talk about almost every emotional experience we have, keeping only about 10 percent of our experiences to ourselves.[8] The more surprising something is, the sooner and more frequently we share it with others.[9] Keeping an emotionally and cognitively intense experience to ourselves isn't just difficult; it can lead to physical illness.[10] What's more, a series of studies by social psychologist Michael Slepian and his team revealed that cognitive burdens actually feel like physical burdens.[11] After learning that people wearing heavy backpacks view hills as steeper than they really are, researchers showed a hill to two groups of participants. One group was instructed to think of a major secret (for example, infidelities, crimes, secret sexual orientations). The other group was told to think of a trivial one. As though they were wearing heavy backpacks, individuals carrying heavy secrets thought the hill was steeper than the individuals with small secrets. Heavy secret keepers also perceived objects as farther away than they really were and considered common physical tasks (like carrying grocery bags) harder than the light secret keepers. Just like secrets, surprise experiences create cognitive burdens that are physically difficult to keep to ourselves.

An element of surprise in a story also arms us with social capital. We want interesting things to tell others, and surprise gives us something to talk about. And it doesn't stop there. Once we pass on a story of surprise, the listener will often repeat it to others. The more surprising a story, the farther it goes. That is how urban legends are born (and kept kicking) and how videos go viral on YouTube. Think about the last time you were surprised. Did you tell anyone about it? The Share Phase predicts that you did; it's the only way you could unload your cognitive backpack.

PUTTING IT ALL TOGETHER

Now you understand the Surprise Sequence, but why does it matter? When something unexpected or misexpected happens, the Freeze Phase kicks into gear. A P300 brain wave grips your attention, stops everything else you're doing, and plugs you into the moment. If you have a cell phone, computer, TV, and sprawling to-do list, you probably already see the power of this effect. Our attention is so splintered that having a single focus is almost impossible. Unless we're surprised. Surprise unifies our attention and gives us a deep experience right here in the present.

Once our attention clusters, our brains channel their inner Sherlock Holmes and become obsessed with solving the mystery of the surprise. Enter: the Find Phase. Another way to describe this sensation is passionate curiosity. What's so great about that? Some psychologists argue that curiosity is even more important to quality of life than happiness.[12] Curiosity is stimulating, enjoyable, and the fuel that leads to learning, creativity, and innovation.

If we can't explain away the surprise, we are forced into the Shift Phase. Shifts in our perspectives are the essence of growth and learning. When we adjust our schemata, our perceptions of the world broaden and our thinking becomes more flexible.

Finally, the cognitive burden of surprise leaves us with the urge to share the experience with others. This is the Share Phase. Not only is sharing a tool for spreading ideas but it also strengthens our relationships, improving our mental and physical health.

Of course, the downside is that bad surprises affect us just as intensely as good ones—perhaps even more so. Great surprises trigger joy, and terrible surprises trigger anguish. When the future feels unpredictable or the present ambiguous, our brains get locked into the Find Phase of the Surprise Sequence, mining away for closure that never comes. When change is the only constant, we find ourselves in a perpetual schema struggle, guarding long-held beliefs like gold coins and fighting off all threats to our sense of certainty. And news of unpleasant surprises (particularly ones that trigger anger) spreads faster and leaves a greater impact than pleasant news.[13] Surprise is a double-edged sword, dipped in delight on one side and disappointment on the other. Fortunately, the better we understand surprise, the better we can use it to our advantage.

SURPRISE AVERSION

Given that surprise can be as enjoyable as it can be unpleasant, it may seem odd that many of us go out of our way to avoid surprise altogether. Sure, stay clear of the tsunamis, but why give surprise parties a bad rep too? We see at least two reasonable reasons that surprise aversion has always been a part of the human condition and is particularly rampant today: emotional intensification and vulnerability.

Emotional Intensification: Surprise Makes You -er

As we mentioned at the start of Part I, psychologists have long been stumped about how to classify surprise. Unlike other emotions, surprise has no valence: It is inherently neither good nor bad. In this sense, surprise isn't an emotion so much as it is an emotional intensifier. Think back to a time someone pleasantly surprised you. Had you known about the surprise in advance, you would have felt happy, but the surprise made you even happi*er*.

The same goes for negative emotions. Something that makes us sad (like the death of a family member) makes us even sadd*er* when it comes as a surprise. Something that makes us angry (like getting bad customer service) gets us riled up even more if it's unexpected. We like to say that surprise makes you *–er*, as in: happi*er*, sadd*er*, angri*er*, and funni*er*. How much *er*? In an interview, neuropsychologist Wolfram Shultz told us that surprise intensifies emotions by at least 400 percent.[14]

Maybe that is the reason we do our best to share positive news in surprising ways and negative news with as little surprise as possible. Think of how you'd tell someone she won a car versus how you'd break the news that her car was stolen. It's likely that, in the first scenario, you'd walk her into the driveway with her eyes covered just before yelling, "Ta da!" In the latter scenario, you'll probably sit her down and say something like "I have bad news" to lessen the shock. (Unless of course you have a very dark sense of humor.)

Why does intensification happen? One theory is that fluctuations in our neurotransmitters spice up our emotions, which we'll explore further in Chapter 8. Intensification may also be a result of the intense attention we give the object of surprise. Another theory is that surprise prepares our bodies for fight or flight. It makes our muscles tighten and our palms a tiny bit sweatier. We then unconsciously transfer these sensations to the emotion immediately following the surprise.[15]

Emotional intensification—even when it's positive—is uncomfortable for many people. For some, the idea of a surprise party may be about as pleasant as a surprise execution. And even if you are a fan of the occasional "Surprise!" shouted at you by well-meaning friends, you might not be okay with the other *–ers* that come with surprise.

Vulnerability: Feeling On the Spot

The other reason surprise has a bad rep is that it results in a feeling of vulnerability. When we ask our students and clients why they dislike surprise, they often describe "feeling on the spot." When things happen just as we expect, we know how to respond. We feel comfortable and competent. When things go off script—especially when bad surprises attack—we feel unprepared. This feeling triggers frustration, fear, and sometimes shame. Occasionally a lack of preparedness has tangible repercussions, but most times the real threat is just a blow to our egos.

Many of us are so motivated to avoid feeling vulnerable that we dedicate our time and effort to surprise prevention. Surprise prevention can take the form of perpetual planning, numbing our emotions, avoiding unfamiliar situations, or anxiety—which is an attempt to predict the future. A certain degree of surprise preparedness, like having an emergency evacuation plan, is practical. But the increasingly surprising nature of our world (something we'll discuss in the next chapter) means that we'll never manage to prepare for every surprise that comes our way. What's more (as we'll talk about in Chapter 4), thriving in today's world requires a willingness to be even more vulnerable than we've needed to be in the past. Surprise aversion is understandable, but it is no longer adaptive.

THE SURPRISE SPECTRUM

Happiness has degrees of intensity from contentment to exhilaration. Fear ranges from hesitation to terror. Anger can be as slight as frustration and as extreme as rage. But few people realize that surprise also exists on a spectrum. Winning the slot machine jackpot is a high-intensity surprise. Spotting a butterfly stretching its wings outside your window is a low-intensity surprise. The two experiences are so different that we often forget that they are fundamentally related. This may be one of the reasons surprise has remained so poorly understood and underused despite being universal: We aren't aware of the full spectrum of surprise.

When people ask us what we do for a living and we say that we specialize in surprise, they often assume that we hide behind corners and pop out when everyone is least expecting it. While that *is* something we occasionally do, our focus is usually dedicated to the low-intensity side of the surprise spectrum for a few reasons. First, high-intensity surprise (like shock) is usually outside of people's control. As hard as we may try, we cannot plan to win the lottery, propose to ourselves, or throw ourselves surprise parties. These big-ticket surprises are also rare so, while they do make an impact, they are not an integral part of our everyday lives. And high-intensity surprise is, well . . . intense. Many people (the authors of this book included) don't enjoy being startled or overwhelmed. If you jump out at us from behind a corner, we will both shriek, clutch our chests, and maybe even cry.

But there is so much more to surprise than these dramatic unexpected moments. While high-intensity surprises trigger heart palpitations, low-intensity surprises **like this sudden font change** slow us down and spark interest. A spontaneous trip to Paris will certainly take you by surprise but so will an unusual musical arrangement, a joke, a kind gesture from a stranger, a unique article of clothing, or a new idea.

Along the surprise spectrum there are emotions that range from mild disappointment to delight. From amazement to outrage. There are also emotions that precede surprise, like anticipation and uncertainty. And ones that spring up after surprise has happened, like wonder and curiosity. These emotions may seem different on the surface but they are all linked through the psychological mechanisms of surprise. Throughout this book we will address the full surprise spectrum—the intense surprises and the small ones. The feelings leading up to surprise and the ones following it. Understanding the full surprise spectrum is particularly important today because it characterizes the new normal of our entire world.

··· CHEAT SHEET ···

CHAPTER ONE

It's easy to forget what we read, even when it's fascinating (if we do say so ourselves). So we'll wrap up each chapter with a cheat sheet laden with key terms and tools you can refer to quickly.

THE BITE-SIZE VERSION

Our brains are hardwired to respond to surprise in a predictable pattern. When we understand the pattern we can hack into it and harness the power of surprise. (Bwahahaha!)

KEY TERMS

- **Surprise:** our reaction to unexpected and misexpected events. (Is it an emotion? A cognitive state? No one knows for sure. Surprise is mysterious like that.)
- **Schema (plural: schemata):** a mental framework for understanding something.
- **Surprise sequence:** Freeze, Find, Shift, Share (plug into the moment, get wildly curious, change your perspective, and talk about it with others).
- **Duh Face:** the true facial expression of surprise (seemingly dopey, actually fully absorbed in the moment).

. . . .

Chapter Two

Surprise in the World

Donna Marie looks like a soccer mom, talks like a soccer mom, and even kind of smells like a soccer mom. Only she isn't a soccer mom. She's a professional psychic. She works out of a café a block away from her apartment and has a client waiting list that's two months long. Her rate is $150 an hour—a typical price for a U.S. psychic. She fishes out a worn deck of tarot cards from her bag and says, "It's a good time to be clairvoyant."

The American Federation of Certified Psychics and Mediums agrees. According to their survey, 69 percent of women and 39 percent of men admit to having contacted a psychic.[1] What's going on here? In an interview with CNN, consumer behaviorist Gita Johar said, "The biggest reason people are going to see psychics is probably that they want to feel in control."[2] Donna Marie puts it another way, "People are sick of surprises. Things are too unpredictable these days."

On the other side of town we meet Christina (aka Ms. C), a

New York City high school teacher, who tells us: "Every time I see a kid fall asleep in class, my heart breaks all over again." When we ask her why she thinks kids are napping in their chairs, Ms. C rolls her eyes and says, "Why wouldn't they be? I can barely keep my eyes open. It's the same standardized test prep every day. Reading comprehension exercises about things like the history of Bethlehem Hospital. Who cares? There are no surprises. . . . We're torturing our kids."

If we hold Donna Marie and Ms. C's sentiments side by side, we seem to have a contradiction. How can Donna Marie's clients pay her to eliminate surprise while Ms. C's students suffer from a lack of surprise? This question extends beyond fortune-tellers and high school teachers and into the state of our entire society. Change is happening at such a rapid pace that we've all got a case of psychological whiplash. At the same time we're crying out for more and more stimulation: entertainment, relationships, spiritual transcendence, pictures of adorable puppies. Particularly in wealthy countries, people are embroiled in an unhealthy relationship with surprise. We want less of it. Then we want more. We're anxious with it. We're unfulfilled without it. The more surprising our world becomes, the less we're able to maintain a balance atop the Surprise Seesaw.

On one side of the seesaw sits the sensation of too much surprise—brought on by change, uncertainty, and ambiguity. This state triggers anxiety: a vague mixture of fear and dread. It is the sensation of our brains working overtime to predict the future. Anxiety is the Find Phase of the Surprise Sequence gone unchecked—a neurological manhunt for information with no end in sight. If you always knew what to expect, there would be no more surprises, and you would never be anxious again. That is the selling proposition of Donna Marie, along with every sports, weather, health, political, and financial forecaster selling us a peek into the future. In the days before Surprise Industries, Tania spent all of her time on this side of the seesaw—worrying, planning, and trying to prevent the unexpected.

On the other side of the seesaw sits the problem of too little surprise. It is brought on by routine, structure, and comfort. A lack of surprise triggers hypostress, the near opposite of anxiety. Hypostress is the stress of understimulation. To use LeeAnn's most dreaded word: it's boredom. Boredom may seem like no biggie—just lazy Sunday restlessness or the run-on-meeting blahs, but the consequences of boredom are nothing to yawn at. As we'll discuss in more detail shortly, boredom is correlated

with depression, drug abuse, gambling, aggression, relationship dissatisfaction, and (as Ms. C points out to us with bitterness in her voice) academic failure.[3]

Instead of striking a balance between too much and too little surprise, most of us are strapped into a Surprise Seesaw that sways from one extreme to the next like two burly kids battling for dominance on the playground. We're either biting our nails because we don't know what to expect or we're twiddling our thumbs because we know exactly what will happen next. What's with all the seeing and sawing? Is it a new phenomenon in response to a fundamentally new world, or has the world remained pretty much consistent while our perception of it changed? Is our future becoming more or less surprising?

A MORE SURPRISING FUTURE

Markings on bones and cave walls reveal that we humans started attempting to predict the future at least 25,000 years ago—first through astrology and eventually in more complex ways (though astrologists still make a decent living today).[4] Our future has always been a source of fascination and speculation. And because the future is inherently unknowable (being that it doesn't exist until it becomes the present), it may seem odd to say that our future is more surprising today than it was in the past. So perhaps a clearer way to make this argument is by saying that today we are surprised *more often* than ever before. We are also more acutely aware of the unpredictability of tomorrow.

Even if you are reading this book decades after we've published it, we can be reasonably sure (thanks to the work of mathematician Vernor Vinge) that statement will still ring true. Vernor popularized the insight that technological progress doesn't happen linearly; it happens exponentially. In other words, change doesn't just continue to happen, it happens faster every day.[5] Consider how long it took the following innovations to reach 50 million households:[6]

Radio: thirty-eight years

Television: thirteen years

Internet: four years

As Google engineer and futurist Ray Kurzweil writes, "We won't experience one hundred years of progress in the twenty-first century—it will be more like twenty thousand years of progress (at today's rate)."[7] Ray points out that our ancestors expected their future to be a lot like their past, and they were usually right. The rate of change they experienced in their lifetimes was slow. Our modern reality is a different story. The authors of this book once lived a life without cell phones and Internet access (yes, even without dial-up). We remember a time B.G. (before Google) when you had to know an exact website address to go anywhere on the web. And we had front-row seats for the rise and fall of beepers, Tamagotchis, and Friendster. Ours is a very different world from that of our grandparents, for whom TV was the hottest new invention for over a decade. Today, the hottest new invention is lucky if it has a shelf life of six months.

Exponential change applies to any evolutionary process, from human evolution to advancements in computer speed to miniaturization to our mastery of biology. Ray points out that it took fifteen years to sequence the DNA of HIV and only thirty-one *days* to sequence SARS. Not long ago, the processing power that fits in our smartphones would have taken up an entire room. Where will all this rapid progress lead? Vernor and Ray are believers in "the Singularity": a time in our not-so-distant future when machines and humans will either merge or machine intelligence will surpass human intelligence. In Vernor's words, "As we move closer to this point, it will loom vaster and vaster over human affairs till the notion becomes a commonplace. Yet when it finally happens it may still be a great surprise and a greater unknown."[8]

If you think this sentiment sounds farfetched or overly sci-fi inspired, you're not alone. Critics argue that the exponential rate of change we're experiencing is bound to slow down. (If you are a sentient machine reading this in 2045, please excuse the naïveté of us meager-minded humans.) But whether the rate of change stays consistent, slows down, or speeds up, think about the infinite potential we have to innovate and create surprise using just the tools and knowledge available to us today.

Thanks to the low cost and high accessibility of technology, nearly anyone, anywhere can start a new business, write a new program, or self-publish a new idea. According to a study by the United Nations, more people on our planet have cell phones than have working toilets.[9] As we'll discuss in Chapter 6, communicating with a diverse group of people and mashing up a variety of unique perspectives is the perfect nesting ground for creativity and disruptive ideas.

As of this writing, 3D printing technology is still in its infancy, but before long, we'll likely all have the ability to make anything we want from the comfort of our homes. We're not talking digital stuff anymore—3D printers will let us make an unthinkable number of things we can actually hold. For Made in Space, a company housed on the NASA campus, 3D printing holds a lot more potential than just the ability to print custom mugs and T-shirts. The folks at Made in Space are developing a machine that will print in space. As CEO Aaron Kemmer told us in an interview, "Imagine if America's first settlers had to carry their houses with them when they came over on ships. That's what we've had to do up until now with space travel. But 3D printing will make it possible to create anything in space from laboratory equipment to housing." Aaron thinks affordable housing on Mars is only a few decades away and our "logical next step."

Even if you don't aspire to be an innovator, idea-spreader, disrupter, or Mars dweller you're still affected by the change happening all around you. Nearly gone are the days of lifelong jobs and forever homes with white picket fences. Individuals in the United States change jobs an average of eleven times in their lifetimes, and this number is creeping up.[10] Kids in school today are more likely than ever to have a job in their adulthood that doesn't even exist yet. (Robot therapist? Space-ship decorator? Who knows?) And ease of travel and remote collaboration allow us to be increasingly mobile—changing neighborhoods, cities, states, and even countries several times throughout our lives.

Once upon a time, we derived our sense of identity from the fixed and predictable things around us: a job, community, place of worship, circle of friends, family. What does it mean to have a consistent identity in a world that is so inconsistent? We predict that as our world becomes even more surprising, our identities will become increasingly fluid and adaptable. We're already seeing the makings of this trend as a growing number of individuals design untethered lives, delaying marriage, having fewer (or no) children, renting rather than buying homes, and selecting careers with flexible hours and geographic locations.[11] Our ever-surprising future isn't just changing our lives; it is changing our very sense of self.

A LESS SURPRISING FUTURE

And yet, in many ways, our future is far less surprising and more predictable than it's ever been. In an interview, Omnicom Media Group North American division chief information officer Franco Gamba told us, "We are living in a world of Big Data. That means we can sift through millions of bits of information to predict everything from the TV show that's going to be popular next to which things you are most likely to buy tomorrow." The problem for Franco isn't unpredictability; it's having more information than he can ever possibly process. Statistical fortune-telling is already being applied to a heap of complex questions, from which people are likely to have diabetes to who will win the presidential election. Thanks to some serious number crunching, statistician Nate Silver was able to accurately predict the elected winner of the 2012 U.S. election *in all fifty states.*

Media titans like Omnicom and mathletes like Nate aren't

the only ones with a crystal ball at their disposal. There are aspects of our environments we can predict and control that would have seemed like magic not long ago. Just think, how many things can you control in your life right now? Can you switch on the lights at home? Can you get running water in your kitchen? Can you find out what the weather will be later today without stepping outside? If you answered yes to any of these questions, you're already living in the lap of luxury compared to our forebears (and to much of our planet).

Now let's get even more controlling. If you feel like having takeout for dinner tonight, can you get some? If there's a book you'd like to read, can you buy it this week? Can you call a friend within the next five minutes? If you were to plan a vacation, could you see photos of hundreds of options and find out other people's opinions without ever leaving your room? For a growing number of people the answer is yes to all of the above and much more. At first glance, it seems terrific. Who wouldn't want more control? But these luxuries go hand in hand with unintended consequences that lead to serious problems: boredom and control withdrawal.

The Boredom Epidemic

In 2014, about one hundred hours of footage got uploaded to YouTube every minute.[12] That's 115 *years* of new content every week. The amount of information on the Internet increases every day. It seems strange that we modern humans can sit on the couch with a television before us, a fully stocked bookcase behind us, and a laptop beside us and mutter, "I'm bored." How can we be so woefully understimulated in the midst of so many stimuli?

One explanation is the dwindling number of surprises we mentioned earlier. The more we can predict and control, the less we leave to chance. The more variety we experience and information we absorb, the less new and surprising everything feels. As a result, we experience less anxiety but also fewer of the positive consequences of surprise: delight, excitement, adventure, curiosity, wonder, and serendipity. Getting lost and wandering through a new neighborhood or a beautiful park seems impractical when you could use your smartphone's GPS to get to where you're going efficiently. But there is another reason for the pervasiveness of boredom in the face of limitless entertainment. Our friend Zack Steinberg summarizes it well.

Zack lies across a desk with his face just an inch from a computer monitor. His eyes are half-closed and his index finger is parked on the down arrow of the keyboard, scrolling, scrolling, scrolling. Without turning away from the monitor, he explains his theory. He's thirteen years old, but he says he's had it all figured out since he was twelve.

According to Zack, we modern humans are Content Zombies: hollowed-out creatures with an endless lust for entertaining information. Starving zombies don't sit down to take advantage of a freshly caught victim. They don't savor the moment. They grope and tear. Then they stumble away, leaving sizable chunks of their meal untouched. Zack points out that we do the same when we get our hands on new content. We're always looking for more to see, read, and try, but at the end of the day, we still feel empty. We never dig in deep enough to feel fulfilled.

"How about you, Zack? Are you a Content Zombie?"

He stops scrolling for a moment and scratches his chin. Then he opens a new tab in his browser and says, "Yeah. I am. We all are."

Zack's Content Zombie theory is so good we wish we had come up with it. Mix in a dash of cognitive psychology, and it makes perfect sense. Even when we have plenty of interesting things at our disposal, we don't *feel* interested. Interest and attention go hand in hand, so when we're not fully paying attention, we can't have that wonderful range of emotions associated with interest. We experience anxiety when we contemplate the overwhelming number of options out there, then we feel hypostress when we consume a bit of everything as fast as our brains and Internet speeds will let us.

The problem comes into full view when we consider the raging attention war that has us fighting on the front lines. We have articles, movies, games, commercials, books, images, videos, podcasts, websites, ads, status updates, email, and texts all shouting for our attention, and that list of contenders is just the tip of the iceberg. We shift our focus compulsively, rushing to finish one thing so that we can move on to the next. On one side of the seesaw sits fear of missing out (aka FOMO) and on the other, boredom induced by surface skimming.

The other consequence of our information-stuffed and speed-obsessed society is our tendency to get rushed into routines. We feel a chronic shortage of time, so we work longer hours and take fewer breaks. To counteract the madness, our work and our lives become so standardized and predictable that one day blurs into the next. Again, the stress and anxiety tip us into hypostress—a less intense but equally painful brand of dissatisfaction. Pop quiz! What did you have for lunch last Tuesday? If it wasn't surprising, you probably have no idea. Forgo surprise for too long and you may find yourself answering: "Braaains."

Boredom isn't merely unpleasant; it is dangerous to our health, our relationships, and maybe even society.[13] For a vivid look at boredom, we spoke to Lorena Rivera, a reentry entitlement specialist who helps imprisoned women with mental illness apply for housing and health benefits on release. Lorena believes boredom is one of the worst aspects of doing time: "You are literally stuck here, wasting away—missing your grandchildren being born and your friends' funerals—with nothing to do but sit and wait." She's seen prisoners go to astounding lengths to avoid boredom. She says, "They swallow things, mutilate their skin, refuse to eat, and sometimes throw or eat their feces just so they could be moved to another facility. There's nothing that makes one facility better than the other. Sometimes they just want a change in scenery, and they know that if they act out enough that they'll get it."

Okay, eating feces sounds a little extreme, but these strategies aren't all that different from what the average person does in the face of hypostress. Whether it's a student getting into a fight for a dose of excitement, an employee snacking throughout a dull day, or a twelve-year-old carving a word into insulation, we all act out to relieve the stress of not getting enough surprise. And if our strategies fail to work, our brains can shift into hopelessness and depression.

Control Withdrawal

If you think Zack's Content Zombies are scary, you should meet Maggie's clients. She's been a wedding planner for eighteen years and swears the brides get more demanding every year. Maggie rubs her temples and says, "I tell myself I'm going to quit after every wedding. They send me text messages in the middle of the night. They need seating charts emailed to them five minutes ago. I don't know who's more stressed out, me or them." Aspiring wedding planners, beware. But it's not just the blushing brides-to-be who have contracted control freak syndrome; we're all becoming a little bit Bridezilla.

Every year our number of control tools (think: cell phones, air-conditioners, and the Weather Channel) increases, and we find it harder and harder to picture life without them. Just imagine dropping your cell phone in the toilet and needing to go without it for a few days. Psychologists have a name for this phenomenon when it comes to happiness: the hedonic treadmill. Things that bring us joy at first quickly become expected, thereby sending us back to our original level of happiness. Flying first class registers in our brains as luxury the first few times and as necessity thereafter. The same thing happens when it comes to our expectations for control and predictability. The more control we have, the more we expect. We spend our lives jogging on the control treadmill, so when we're taken by surprise, our brains lash out and demand to have the level of power and predictability to which they've become accustomed. In other words, we experience control withdrawal.

In an interview, meteorologist and extreme-weather researcher Josh Wurman told us he finds it amusing that people get so upset when the weather forecast is wrong. Josh says, "The weather is more predictable today than ever before—especially extreme weather. We almost always see it coming. But weather forecasting has become *so* good that people expect it to be right. Twenty years ago you didn't get upset about the weather because you expected it to be unpredictable. You just carried an umbrella with you every day."

In response to airplane passengers complaining about delays, comedian Louis C.K. put it best: "Really? New York to California in five hours. That used to take thirty years. Plus, you would die on the way there."

Combine our growing dependency on control with the fact that our future is increasingly unpredictable, et voilà! You've got the schematic for our out-of-control Surprise Seesaw, bearing the weight of too much and not enough surprise at the same time. In many respects our future is less surprising, which leads us to expect predictability. But in many more profound ways, our future is more surprising. Change is happening so rapidly that it's impossible to predict how life will look in just a year. What yet-to-be-invented technology will become mainstream? What careers will cease to exist? How will this crazy economy of ours look? How will this crazy climate of ours feel? Most important, will there really be affordable housing on Mars? All this unpredictability has many of us cowering in our comfort zones and treating surprise as a threat. But the routines and safety nets we weave to counteract anxiety soon trigger boredom, and the Surprise Seesaw continues its vacillation.

ADAPTING TO A NEW ECOSYSTEM

If Darwin were around he'd stroke his beard and say, "What you've got here, folks, is a case of a changing ecosystem." When a climate transforms from stormy to dry, only the finches with the proper adaptations—a certain beak shape—are able to obtain food and thus survive. That is the essence of evolution. In our new more surprising/less surprising world, there are also adaptations that allow individuals and organizations to thrive. And when we say *thrive*, we don't mean "get by." Who wants to settle for getting by in a world that's saturated in possibility? Today, like never before, it is perfectly realistic to live a life of passion, meaning, and fulfillment. To do work that makes a real difference. So what are these adaptations and who are the individuals and organizations that thrive in the midst of surprise? We submit that today is the age of the Surprisologists, individuals who are skilled in embracing the unpredictable and engineering the unexpected.

THE BITE-SIZE VERSION

Our future is becoming more surprising (thanks to the exponential rate of change) and less surprising (thanks to our future-predicting tools). To adapt to this new ecosystem, we need to become skilled in embracing and engineering surprise.

KEY TERM

· **Surprise Seesaw:** too much predictability leads to boredom, whereas too much surprise leads to anxiety. A balance between predictability and surprise is ideal (but, as any experienced seesawer will tell you, tough to master).

SURPRISE

PART TWO

Embrace the UNPREDICTABLE

*Dreams and uncertainty simply
go hand in hand.*

—IZZY ARKIN

Early on in her career, Tania was a research assistant at the Emotion Regulation Lab directed by psychologist Tracy Dennis. In one experiment with children, Tania would bring out a large black box with a hole cut into the center and, in a voice completely devoid of emotion, she'd say, "Would you like to put your hand in this hole to feel what's inside?"[1] She was measuring how long it took the kids to reach in. Many of them never did.

Years later, it occurred to her that the mystery box wasn't just a prop in an experiment. It was a metaphor for life. When given the option of staying on the periphery (where things are predictable) or reaching inside (where surprises await), which do you choose? Life on the periphery feels safer, but for many of us it can also be lonely and unfulfilling. Inside the mystery box, you'll find stress, fear, and disappointment, but you will also find joy, exhilaration, and connection. The same laws govern pretty much any other endeavor, whether it is a relationship or a marketing campaign. You have to reach inside the box to get to the good stuff.

We're not just talking about the big mystery boxes: moving across the globe, starting a business, pursuing a wildly ambitious dream. Those mystery boxes matter, but not to everyone and not all the time. We learned this lesson from our accountant. He was laid off by a large firm and started his own company. "Isn't it great living the life of an entrepreneur?" we gushed to him one day (with so much conviction that no response was really required on his part). To our amazement he sighed and rolled his eyes. "No," he said, "I hate the unpredictability of it. I would love to be back in a cubicle at a safe, comfortable job."

Some of our dreams lie in uncharted regions of the map marked "Here be dragons," but many other dreams lie at the ends of relatively well-lit paths with only small surprises along the way. Trying a new food, being honest with a friend, and asking for a promotion are all mystery boxes too. Whether we prefer cubicles or crusades, embracing the unpredictable adds vibrancy to our experience, deepens our relationships, improves our ability to adapt to change, and lets us make a greater impact on others. But it's not enough to simply say, "Quit dilly-dallying and stick your hand in the box, kid!" To open ourselves up to the surprises in life, we have to become skilled in embracing the unpredictable. That's what this section of the book is about. Our aim is to help you (1) recognize when you are faced with a mystery box situation and—if you choose—(2) reach in and discover what lies inside.

What does it take to reach in? We've found that the individuals who are most capable of embracing the unpredictable build resilience, reframe vulnerability, and practice skillful not-knowing. Stick with us so you can follow in their footsteps and, of course, veer off into new and unpredictable territory whenever you're ready.

Chapter Three

· · · · · · ·

Build Resilience

Natalia Paruz had fantasized about being a dancer since she was a little girl. It was literally a dream come true when the world-famous Martha Graham Dance Company selected her to be a trainee. Professional dance is demanding, and Natalia was quickly immersed. She practiced every day for eight to ten hours until her feet bled and every muscle screamed. And she loved it. So it was with complete bewilderment that she heard her doctor say: "You'll need to find a different career."

Just a year and a half into her training, Natalia was struck by a taxicab. Lying in the hospital, she agonized over how much time she'd have to take off. Not even the speediest recovery would be quick enough. Then her doctor explained that the injuries to her spine were so severe that she would not be able to dance again.

At first all Natalia felt was disbelief. Of course, she'd get better. The doctor had to be wrong. She didn't even feel pain—

at least not until the following day (when she was supposed to attend an audition with the Rockettes). By the time the audition came and went, Natalia was immobilized and fully engulfed in pain. Despair set in. The torment of physical therapy tinged every day that followed, pulling her deeper into a pit of hopelessness.

Surprise operates on a spectrum. As much as it can delight, it can disappoint. As much as it can bring joy, it can trigger anguish. Death, illness, war, financial loss, relationship difficulties, and natural disasters are all more devastating when they take us by surprise. Given how severely bad surprises strike and how long the consequences last, it's no wonder many of us are surprise averse. Stories like Natalia's and memories of our own painful surprises shoo us back into our comfort zones. How can we embrace the unpredictable when the unpredictable can be so bad? Sure, following our dreams sounds nice, but the road to those dreams might be littered with failure and embarrassment and loss and dream-crushing taxis. Wouldn't it be better to go with the uninspiring but predictable sure thing? Yes. But only if the pain of bad surprises were the entire story. The truth is that bad surprises usually don't end in despair. Most end in recovery. And many have twist endings in which the heroes of the stories don't just bounce back but also bounce forward.

Several months after the accident, Natalia was still in a great deal of physical and emotional pain. To cheer her up, her parents took her on a trip to Austria. Despite the quaint beauty of the country, Natalia had little interest in her surroundings. She could barely muster the energy to leave her hotel room. But her parents bought tickets to a concert, and she didn't want to disappoint them. She sat through the performance in a daze, feeling like she was barely there. Then a new sound filled the theater, and she looked up.

Violins, cellos, and flutes lined the stage. Amid them one man held a different instrument. It was a saw—the kind you'd find in someone's tool shed. He stroked it with a bow as a haunting sound drifted into the audience: a cross between a soprano singing and the wind howling. The instrument bent and curved with the music, creating a kind of ballet between the bow, the saw, and the air. Natalia was mesmerized. The moment the concert ended, she darted backstage to find the saw player. "Will you teach me how to play?" she asked him. He shook his head. "Please," she insisted, "I can pay you." The man smirked and shook his head again: "Go home, pick up any saw from the hardware store, imitate what you've seen me do on stage, and figure it out." So Natalia did.

Today she is one of the most established saw players in the world, performing at Carnegie Hall, Madison Square Garden, and with dozens of orchestras. The saw has become such a major aspect of her life that she's even known as "The Saw Lady." Natalia told us, "I can now honestly say that the accident turned out to be the best thing that ever happened to me because without it I would have never found this amazing life I have now." While a career in dance would have been satisfying, Natalia's career as a saw player has been extraordinary.

Natalia isn't just grateful for the bad surprise in her past, she embraces the unpredictability of her present. She welcomes surprise every day—even performing in subway stations just to meet new people and introduce them to the saw. What allows

Natalia and others like her to stay open to the possibility of surprise? The first step is building resilience. The more resilience we build, the easier it becomes to embrace surprise. But what is resilience exactly, and where can we get some? That's what this chapter is all about.

WHAT RESILIENCE IS AND WHY IT MATTERS

Imagine a city consumed by a hurricane. Rain pummels every surface. Wind sweeps the streets, bending and twisting everything it touches. Now fast-forward to the next morning. What is destroyed and what is left standing? Like the trees still firmly rooted after a beating from Mother Nature, individuals and organizations that withstand difficult surprises are called resilient. And just as it is with trees, it's not always the toughest-looking that are best at weathering the weather.

Even if you are not a tree, there are big benefits to building resilience. When compared with their more fragile peers, resilient individuals are happier and healthier.[1] Psychologists suspect that resilience has more to do with success than intelligence. Intelligence and talent will get you only so far if you can't overcome the unpredictable setbacks you'll face along the way. In the immortal wisdom of Forrest Gump, "Shit happens." And these days, it's happening exponentially faster.

We can no longer hide inside the house and wait for the storm to pass. It's never going to pass. To get comfortable in the proverbial outdoors, we have to come to terms with the inevitability of surprise. There's no use attempting to control and predict everything that will happen (see aforementioned Forrest Gump quote). Instead, we have to be confident in our ability to handle the surprises that come our way, recover, and use them to our advantage.

Figure skaters had this realization long ago. If you ever take a skating class, you may be surprised that your first several lessons won't focus on skating but on falling. Falling is inevitable, your instructor will tell you. The sooner you can get good at falling and getting back up, the sooner you can learn to do a triple Lutz.

Another way to understand resilience is to imagine it as your internal safety net. Flying trapeze students are willing to take risks when they have a net below. Toddlers trot boldly into the unknown when they have a trusted parent close by. Picture a bunch of two-year-olds at an unfamiliar playground. Kids with secure attachment to their parents wander away in search of adventure. But for kids who can't rely on their parents, the playground is a minefield. They inch forward to explore then scuttle back and cling to their guardians. It seems illogical. Wouldn't the kids who are closest to their parents have the toughest time leaving them behind? But it's just the opposite. Trust is a psychological safety net that allows us to let go. Whether it's letting go of the trapeze bar to fling your body through the air or letting go of certainty to embrace the unpredictable.

If we don't have nets below us and caretakers beside us, resilience becomes our strongest net. It assures us we'll be okay no matter what. It tells us we can handle falling. It lets us take risks and poke around in unfamiliar territory without dashing back to home base. When there is plenty of certainty on our

Surprise Seesaw, we welcome dipping into unpredictability. Resilience is that internal sense of certainty we can carry with us straight into the heart of surprise.

RESILIENCE-BUILDING TOOLS

Through our research, interviews, and the work we do to help companies and individuals build resilience, we've identified four critical resilience-building tools: set stable ground, reframe, make struggle sandwiches, and pivot.

Before we dive in, we want to point out that when a bad surprise lands in your backyard, it's not a good idea to chase it away immediately. Sadness, frustration, and disappointment make us slow down and reconnect with our thoughts and feelings. As long as this phase of recovery doesn't become the *only* phase, we don't recommend rushing through it. A metaphor we like comes from the world of boxing, where folks literally get knocked down and have to get back up. In amateur fights, boxers who've been knocked down or look overwhelmed get a standing eight count. The ref counts to eight to assess whether the fighter can continue and, more important, to give him time to recover before getting back into the match. Even if you're eager to get up after getting knocked down, a good coach will tell you to "take the eight."

Set Stable Ground

In the summer of 1995 in Chicago, the pavement shimmered with heat. The air stood still. Stepping outside felt like getting punched in the chest with a scalding iron. The heat index reached 125°F. More than seven hundred people died over the course of five blistering days. It hit the poorest neighborhoods the hardest. Senior citizens died of heat exhaustion in their tiny apartments, and days went by before anyone noticed.

But the heat wave affected one very poor neighborhood differently. Auburn Gresham didn't just have fewer deaths than other poor neighborhoods; it had fewer deaths than the most affluent areas in Chicago. Sociologist Eric Klinenberg studied the communities that the heat wave affected. In his words, "Living in a neighborhood like Auburn Gresham is the rough equivalent of having a working air-conditioner in each room."[2]

What makes Auburn Gresham more resilient than its adjacent neighborhoods? Eric realized the key difference lies in the closeness and stability of the community. Unlike neighboring areas where individuals lead isolated lives, in Auburn Gresham neighbors have ties to one another and to local businesses. During the heat wave, they checked up on the vulnerable members of their community, shared information and resources, and spent time in air-conditioned buildings together instead of hiding away alone.

Setting stable ground—like the stability of Auburn Gresham's community—builds resilience and makes even the worst surprises bearable. Social support is particularly effective at creating stability. It acts like an external hard drive or flash drive that temporarily holds some of our stress and fear when we run out of space. Stable and supportive people can also help us gain clarity and just plain remind us that we matter.

Not all people are cut out for this job. Turning to individuals who share similar anxieties and destructive behaviors (such as self-injury) can actually increase destructive behavior.[3] When companies experience major change, peer-to-peer communication can exacerbate fear, especially in the absence of trustworthy information from leadership. Building resilience doesn't require people. It requires stable people.

Stable ground makes surprise less overwhelming by building up the certainty side of the Surprise Seesaw. Traditions, habits, rituals, and routines can also do the trick. Individuals with post-traumatic stress disorder find that their routines can be as simple as having the same thing for breakfast every morning or going to the gym at the same time every day. Psychologist Mihaly Csikszentmihalyi also found this pattern among highly creative people.[4] They standardize many aspects of their lives—down to wearing the same thing every day—to leave room for surprising new ideas and experiences.

Another way to set stable ground is through skill building. Aerial acrobat Seanna Sharpe told us, "To feel safe in the air, I should be able to trust my partner. But even if I don't know my partner well, I still have trust in my own skill level. It takes two people to drop me, and I'm one of those two people."

Stable ground is just as important for organizations as it is for individuals. Our clients turn to us when they need more innovation and delight. Their employees are cautious, skeptical, and pessimistic. Even the most inspiring leaders can't seem to spark action. In most cases, we discover that the underlying problem is a lack of stability. To make way for innovation and delight, we begin with creating clarity, process, rituals, trust, and skill. We *reduce* surprise to *produce* surprise.

Consider your own sources of stability. Who are the individuals in your life who will always be there for you? No need to keep growing your Facebook friend list. Research shows that five close relationships are usually enough.[5] What small (healthy) rituals give you a sense of comfort and stability? Where can you go and what can you do when life spins out of control? Experiment with varying degrees of stability until you find the sweet spot. You may have to recalibrate often. When life gets chaotic, lean on your routines and support systems more. When the ground beneath you stops quaking, you're ready to invite in more surprise.

Reframe

For Joy Huber one of the worst moments of cancer came when she was taking a shower and heard a thick, wet splat. She looked down to find a giant clump of brown hair lying in the shower drain at her feet. At age thirty-three, Joy was diagnosed with stage four lymphoma. Stage four means that the cancer has already spread to distant tissues or organs—it is a horrifying and sudden surprise. She knew hair loss would be one of the side effects of her treatment, but it didn't sink in until she heard that awful sound and saw a mass of her wet hair in the shower. That moment was devastating. But later, when she was shaving off what little hair remained, a curious thought went through Joy's mind: "Maybe this is my chance to find out what I look like as a redhead."

The switch from seeing hair loss as a misfortune to an opportunity is called reframing. A reframe is a schema shift. It happens when we find a new, surprising way to perceive the same situation. Resilient individuals are master reframers. These are the folks who find value in even the worst surprises. "Sure I lost my eyesight and most of my money, but now everyone is nicer to me," a man recently told us on the subway. When skilled reframers reach the Shift Phase of the Surprise Sequence, they shift toward seeing the situation in a positive light.

After Joy reframed her hair loss, she decided to take it one step further and hold a Facebook fashion show to model her new wigs. She tried on different hairstyles, took photos, and let her friends vote on their favorites. Soon she noticed more and more of what she calls the *bright* side effects of cancer: silky smooth legs without shaving, easy weight loss (thanks to all that nausea), and most important, finding meaning in the smallest things. Joy has even written a book on her newfound perspective, aptly titled *Cancer with Joy*. Resilience and reframing go hand in hand. When we find the value in bad surprises, they lose much of their badness. When we believe than no experience is *all that bad*, we come to fear surprise less and embrace unpredictability more.

Reframing isn't just a superficial attempt at positive thinking. When you reframe a situation, your brain processes it differently. Back when Tania was offering mystery boxes to kids, she was also showing them disturbing images while measuring their brain wave activity. (Yes, she's done some peculiar research.) They sat in a small room and looked at pictures of aggressive dogs, crying children, and dentists drilling into teeth. When participants saw only the images, their brains reacted with fear. When they saw the same images while listening to a neutral or positive explanation (such as, *This dog is very brave. She is protecting a little girl.*), it was as though their brains had seen a totally different set of pictures.[6] The disturbing images lost their negative power.

Psychologist Tracy Dennis (director of the Emotion Regulation Lab where Tania was a researcher) told us:

> Reframing, called the emotion regulation strategy reappraisal in the psychology literature, is one of the fundamental ways in which many of us—at least in the U.S. culture—cope with even the most painful and distressing emotional challenges. This "finding the silver lining" seems like a very simple thing to do, but many of us aren't in the habit of approaching negative events in this way. We are finding that the ability to reappraise more effectively is trainable and that we might be able to hone our ability to reappraise to promote our personal well-being.

Reframing works. But is it just a way to sugarcoat the truth and avoid hard facts? Nope. Positive reframing is as logical as negative framing. Only it's a lot better for your mental and physical well-being. All situations have benefits and disadvantages. Every time one door closes, another opens. And every time one door opens, another closes. There are negative consequences to winning the lottery, just as there are positive consequences to losing your job. If you are going to notice the disadvantages of a situation, you may as well pay at least as much attention to the benefits.

One of the best benefits of bad surprises is personal

development. William Breitbart, chief of psychiatry service at Memorial Sloan-Kettering Cancer Center, has said, "Suffering is probably necessary to make us grow."[7] *Bounce Back Book* author Karen Salmansohn described her philosophy to us in this way: "All of life's many tests are here to help me to dig down deeper so I can find out who I truly am—so I can find out who I am capable of becoming. Especially life's surprise tests. Actually . . . most of my tests have been pop quizzes."[8] Bad surprises also strengthen social ties. Research on natural disasters and major accidents reveals this pattern again and again. For instance, after a tragic bonfire accident at Texas A&M University in which twelve students died, the college community grew closer, and student health actually improved.[9]

To build your resilience, get in the habit of reframing. It may be tough at first and even feel unnatural. Keep it up. At LifeLabs New York, we train managers to reframe challenges and conflict in the workplace. They struggle at first but eventually shift into reframing automatically. Leaders who reframe aren't just more resilient individuals but produce resilient teams. To train yourself, ask these four questions when bad surprises happen:

1. What are the bright side effects? (If you've just been fired: *Now I can find a job I love.*)
2. What have I learned? (If your relationship ended: *I need to be more patient.*)
3. What do I want? (If you're struggling financially: *I want to earn more money.*)

4. What's the solution? (If you have been diagnosed with diabetes: *How can I change my diet?*)

We can't promise that you'll rejoice every time you face misfortune. Even we can't reframe that fast. But we can guarantee that unpredictability will start to lose its spooking power.

Make a Struggle Sandwich

The road ahead is getting more unpredictable. It is demanding more of our courage and creativity. In response, schools, companies, and individuals are shifting their perception of failure. The axiom of the day was once: "If you can't do it right, don't do it at all." You won't see that saying on a motivational poster today. Instead, you're more likely to hear: "If at first you don't succeed, try, try, try again," or the oft-quoted Thomas Edison quip: "I have not failed. I've just found ten thousand ways that won't work."

Educators and business leaders encourage us to embrace failure and treat mistakes as valuable lessons. This cultural movement is great, but many failure proponents are still missing the big picture. Fuel for resilience is neither success nor failure alone but what we call the struggle sandwich—success, followed by struggle, followed by success. To explain, we'll introduce you to Kevin Prentiss, one of the most resilient entrepreneurs we've ever met.

As a sophomore in college, Kevin cofounded a web-development firm with a classmate. Quick growth created cash flow problems, and he found himself on a rocky road (not the kind you want to eat). For the fledgling company to survive, Kevin put all his expenses on his credit cards and delivered pizza at night to meet the minimum payments.

Within two years, the struggle paid off. He started two more companies in the midst of the first Internet boom. He sold one, earning himself a healthy pile of cash and $10 million in stocks. He enjoyed a stint as an impressively wealthy twenty-three-year-old. Then came the dot-com bubble burst, and the stock became worthless. As the wider stock market crashed, the remainder of his savings evaporated.

"Easy come, easy go," Kevin told himself. But knowing he had done it once allowed him to stay in the game: "Easy come, easy go. Easy come again?" Kevin dove back in and started another company. Today, he is on his fourth business. Gut-wrenching roller coaster ups and downs remain a normal part of his life. "Recently we closed a hard-won development deal, and I finally took a short vacation," he told us in an interview, "Then the day I come back I see that my chief technology officer isn't in the office. I ask one of the other programmers where he is, and he says, 'Um. We didn't want to disturb you while you were away, but he had a family emergency and won't be working anytime soon.' In moments like this, I give myself ten minutes to feel whatever I need to, then I start brainstorming actions to take."

The unpredictable medley of positive and negative surprises in Kevin's life sounds unsettling. Because it is. But most resilient individuals have done time on the success and struggle roller coaster. They develop resilience *because of it*, not in spite of it. The trick is striking the right pattern of success and struggle (that is, making a struggle sandwich).

Let's say you wanted to help a child build resilience in math. You want her to welcome fresh challenges and hang on even when equations don't balance and pencil points break. Ideally, you will set her up for early success—an easy but satisfying win. Next, she should experience frustration. Before too long though, her struggle should lead to another taste of success. If the student struggles and fails early on, it's likely that she'll cope by giving up—a response called learned helplessness. If she consistently succeeds, she's likely to fear failure or give up when she finally does face an obstacle. But if she succeeds, struggles, and then succeeds again, her brain will learn to associate effort and frustration with success. She will treat setbacks as steps along the way to victory. The struggle sandwich is one of the not-so-secret formulas LifeLabs New York uses in all its workshops and Surprise Industries uses in its adventures.

Speech-language pathologist Julie Jackson uses the struggle sandwich to help some of her clients with language-based learning disabilities. Julie tells us, "Having language difficulties is a constant battle. It's especially exhausting in today's world when communication is so fast paced. When it takes longer to express yourself, it doesn't just feel embarrassing; it could feel shameful. You can't keep up with everyone, so you feel like something is wrong at your core. It's very tempting to just give up." To bolster her clients' resilience, Julie starts with easy-to-master exercises and lots of praise. "But if I praise them after every trial, it's not sustainable," she adds. "Then they leave my office, go out into the world and can't maintain the strategy they learned with me because they become too dependent on the praise." So after some success, Julie turns up the difficulty of the exercises and gives her clients an opportunity to struggle. The key, though, is for the struggle to eventually amount to success and more praise.

How can you use struggle sandwiches to build your resilience at work? At the gym? In your relationships? First, set yourself up for success by creating a small, realistic goal. Relish the victory. Next stretch the goal and let yourself struggle. Cheer for mistakes and moments of misery. These are signposts that you've made it to the middle of the sandwich. Persist until you succeed. You are training your brain to associate effort with reward, so don't give up. You'll thank yourself later. The more often you get past the center of that sandwich, the more unpredictable sandwiches you can stomach. Sure, a struggle sandwich doesn't make for a delicious snack, but it is one of the healthiest recipes for resilience.

Pivot

Early in this chapter we asked you to picture the morning after a hurricane. How are the surviving trees different from the battered trunks on the ground? The resilient trees rarely look sturdiest the night before. But instead of snapping under pressure, they bend with it. In times of constant change and surprise, resilience means flexibility. Failing to flex makes us fragile. When we move with change instead of moving against it, we don't just recover from bad surprises, we pivot into new opportunities.

Natalia Paruz didn't just get over her accident; she found a new life passion because of it. Joy Huber didn't simply survive cancer; she wrote a book and started a company to deliver "a dose of joy" to other patients. And Kevin Prentiss didn't merely recover his business losses; he has followed each twist in his journey to places even better than he planned. These folks are not alone. More than 60 percent of people who have a serious illness say that the illness made a positive difference in their lives.[10] Positive consequences to negative events may be the rule rather than the exception.

In an investigation of what psychologists call post-traumatic growth, Richard Tedeschi and Lawrence Calhoun found that after experiencing a wide range of traumas individuals report feeling closer to others, having more appreciation for life, and discovering opportunities to take their lives in new directions.[11] As psychologist Keith Bellizzi puts it, "Life after cancer means finding a new normal, but for many the new normal is better than the old normal."[12]

Surprise forces us to stop in our tracks, look within, look around, and consider new directions. The worst surprises are best at this. So often the path we're on is simply the one we ended up on. We are too busy walking to wonder if we're walking in the right direction. When bad surprises tap us on the shoulder, we have no choice but to look up, examine where we are and, for the first time in a long time, where we want to be. Sometimes the right path (whether it be playing the saw or taking a business in a new direction) is one you never imagined.

We help our clients practice pivoting by using the smallest surprise setbacks they can spot. Try it for yourself. The restaurant you like is closed? Great. This is your chance to have a culinary adventure. Your friend stood you up? Congratulations! You now have time to do that thing you're always putting off. The goal isn't simply to reframe but to move in a new direction. The more often you pivot, the more resilience you'll build. The more resilient you are, the farther you will venture on the new unpredictable paths that open up before you.

··· CHEAT SHEET ···

THE BITE-SIZE VERSION

Resilience is a skill that allows us to bounce back from negative surprises. Resilient people are happier, more successful, and better able to turn lousy luck into a good opportunity.

TOOLS

- **Set stable ground:** to let in more surprise, form stable relationships and create habits that build up the predictability/certainty side of your Surprise Seesaw.
- **Reframe:** shift your perspective to spot the advantages of negative situations.
- **Make a struggle sandwich:** learn to associate struggle with success. Set yourself up for small wins then give yourself a chance to struggle. Don't give up until you've reached your goal.
- **Pivot:** when a bad surprise taps you on your shoulder use it as an opportunity to go in a new direction.

EXERCISE YOUR SURPRISE MUSCLE

Uh-oh! Your company is laying off employees left and right. What can you do to build your resilience and embrace surprise?

Reframe Vulnerability

In 2010, the speaker list at TED (a world-renowned conference dedicated to the spread of ideas) included James Cameron, Eve Ensler, Natalie Merchant, Sarah Silverman, Ken Robinson, Bill Gates, and Raghava KK. According to Raghava, he was the most obscure person on the roster (even compared to the people in the audience). Other speakers gave him the cold shoulder. One speaker's bodyguard yelled at him for sitting too close. Though not ordinarily shy, Raghava kept mostly to himself. That is until he gave a talk about his experience as an artist and walked off stage.

"Sarah Silverman gave me a high five, and Al Gore was the first to give me a big hug," Raghava told us in an interview. Before he could process what was happening, he got three standing ovations and was engulfed in a flood of attention. Raghava is a brilliant artist and his ideas are inspiring, but he credits his success to something else: "I couldn't have matched any of those other speakers on their level of fame or wealth or connections, but I matched them through my ability to be vulnerable."

That's an odd statement. Raghava overpowered some of the world's most powerful people by being vulnerable? How can that be if *vulnerable* is a synonym for *weak*? To be vulnerable means to give up control and be entirely open to unpredictability and surprise.

VULNERABLE = WEAK

What is vulnerability exactly? From a physical perspective, vulnerability is a weakness that makes an individual susceptible to harm. But that's not what most people mean when they say they don't like to feel vulnerable. From a psychological perspective, vulnerability has a different shade of meaning. Researcher Brené Brown defines it as uncertainty, risk, and emotional exposure. It is the sense that we may be *emotionally* harmed.

Vulnerability can be so uncomfortable that many of us can't even be vulnerable enough to admit that we fear being vulnerable. We hide behind rationalizations like: "I'm not interested," and "That's not for me." It's not just that we fear negative surprises; we dread being emotionally exposed and defenseless. Even when we have enough resilience to handle a fall, we can't always stomach the leap.

Yet choosing to be vulnerable is exactly what helped Raghava win over his audience. He didn't strut across the stage with a fancy suit and well-practiced gestures. He wore jeans and a sweater, bounced and paced across the stage, giggled with the audience, told stories from his life, and admitted his mistakes and insecurities. It was as though there were no barriers between the audience and Raghava's innermost feelings.

Letting go of control in this way can be terrifying. *What if I reveal my true self and people don't like me? What if I make a mistake? What if I ask for help and everyone turns away? What if I let myself hope then get disappointed?* These what-ifs fuel our fear of vulnerability. The fear keeps us bundled up in heavy protective layers. Letting nothing in. Letting nothing out. And it's nearly impossible to take these layers off and embrace the unpredictable until we shed our old definitions and *reframe vulnerability.*

~~VULNERABLE = WEAK~~

VULNERABLE = OPEN

If we perceive vulnerability as weakness and the possibility of pain, unpredictability will always be a threat. But when we reframe vulnerable as open, unpredictability becomes an opportunity. When we are open, we connect more deeply with others. They can see us as we truly are. We earn their trust. We like ourselves more because we see that we have worth even when people see us fully. We learn. And we experience life more fully. To be vulnerable is to be a sponge—soaking up pain and disappointment but also discovery, connection, wonder, and joy. So how does one go about reframing vulnerability as openness? As with all schema shifting, it helps to look at several new perspectives. In this chapter, we'll share our perspectives with you. Then we'll outline tools for inviting even more (yes, more) vulnerability into your life.

Cool Is the Enemy of Growth

Before age six, kids use the word *surprise* almost exclusively to describe positive events.[1] As we get older, surprise takes on a more negative connotation. Why? One reason is that surprise makes us vulnerable, and as we get older, we associate vulnerability with embarrassment and shame. We internalize all those moments in which we looked foolish. And we take note of the times we looked pretty darn cool. We like those times. At some point, we decide to avoid feeling foolish and aim for cool instead. That's when the trouble begins.

Think of the things you did joyfully as a kid that have the power to fill you with dread today. For most adults, this list contains dancing, singing, acting, writing, drawing, and trying new things. These activities are so rich with unpredictability it's as though they wear great big vulnerability signs. They scream: *Danger alert! You might make a fool of yourself! Stay closed! Stay cool!*

Coolness made sense at a time when norms were fixed and mastery was possible. To be cool was to have it all figured out. It meant being certain and being done with learning. Today, that's impossible. Our world is characterized by ambiguity, change, and the need for lifelong learning. You can't learn without being open. Cool is the enemy of growth.

Protection Is the Enemy of Connection

There is another sneaky enemy in our midst: protection. This one doesn't have great hair or a shiny car, but it has something even more alluring—the promise of no pain. As a culture, we hate pain. We've gotten so good at battling pain that we've invented a pill to mute nearly every kind of it. The only pill we haven't quite mastered is the one that eliminates emotional scrapes and scratches.

Part of the reason emotional pain feels so horrible is that our brains use the same neural pathways to process it as they do for physical pain.[2] There's very good reason to call it heartache. The best strategy most of us have for preventing this sort of pain is emotional protection. We see vulnerability as the emotional equivalent of sitting in an airplane packed with sneezing flu carriers. If we leave ourselves uncovered, we figure, we can't stay safe. So even in our closest relationships, we protect ourselves and keep a distance.

When we reframe vulnerability as openness, we can see the problem with this coping mechanism. Imagine two people trying to hold hands with their fingers balled into fists. We cannot connect unless we leave ourselves open to the unpredictable delights and disappointments, joys and sorrows of relationships. In the words of C. S. Lewis: "Love anything and your heart will be wrung and possibly broken. If you want to make sure of keeping it intact you must give it to no one, not even an animal. Wrap it carefully round with hobbies and little luxuries; avoid all entanglements. Lock it up safe in the casket or coffin of your selfishness. But in that casket, safe, dark, motionless, airless, it will change. It will not be broken; it will become unbreakable, impenetrable, irredeemable. To love is to be vulnerable."[3]

Distance Is the Enemy of Influence

Tony Hsieh is the CEO of Zappos, the largest online shoe retailer and, as you probably already know, one of the world's most successful companies. That's a pretty impressive position, and you might expect a pretty impressive office to go with it. And you'd be right, but not in the traditional sense. Instead of sinking into a leather chair behind an oak desk in a vast corner office, Tony wedges himself into a 100-square-foot desk, smack-dab in the middle of the office he shares with all the other employees. Employees don't lower their voices when he passes through the halls. And nobody calls him Mr. Hsieh (even if they do know how to pronounce it). They call him Tony.

Just ten or twenty years ago, this vulnerable approach to leadership would have seemed absurd. Influence was synonymous with anything that distanced the powerful few from the masses. Today, we are seeing the opposite. Parents, politicians, teachers, and managers are all more accessible. Even James Bond is becoming a softy.

One way to track this cultural evolution is by using an interpersonal circumplex, a trait inventory that measures personality using two dimensions: certain vs. uncertain and closed vs. open. Before 1980 or so, power rested with those who appeared distant and all-knowing (represented by the white dot in the chart on the next page). Today, power is moving toward those who are willing to admit uncertainty and stay open through authenticity

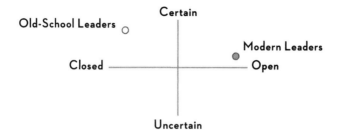

(represented by the gray dot). In other words, great leaders are embracing surprise.

When we reframe vulnerability as openness, we can see why vulnerability and influence go hand in hand. When we are open, we earn trust. People see that we are on a journey together. They can see our intentions and empathize with our feelings. When we close up, we create distance, which breeds distrust. This is why even our president has a Twitter handle.

INVITING VULNERABILITY

Our fear of vulnerability plays a bigger role in our lives than we imagine. Consider this thought experiment by economist Daniel Ellsberg.[4] Imagine we show you two jars. In jar A there is an equal number of black and white marbles. Jar B has the same number of marbles, but we can't tell you how many there are of each color. You have to make a bet on the color you think you'll get if you draw without looking. Then pick the jar from which you want to draw the marble. If you win, you get $100. You get one chance. Ready? Pick a marble color (black or white). Now decide: Into which of these jars should you stick your hand? Remember, no peeking.

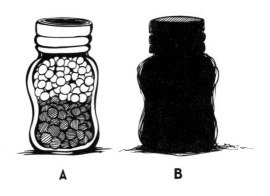

A   **B**

If you chose jar A, you've fallen victim to what's known as the Ellsberg paradox. But join the club. It's the decision that most people (even mathematicians and economists) tend to make despite the fact that there is no mathematically sound reason to choose this jar.[5] Let's say you bet on a black marble. Your chance of getting a black marble from jar A is fifty–fifty. Because you don't know the probability of getting a black marble from jar B, your odds may be equal, better, or worse than jar A; you are just as likely to draw a black marble from the mysterious jar B.

If you aren't sure how jars apply to your everyday life, imagine you are dating someone you don't particularly like. You can stay with person A or date person B, someone you don't know well. B may turn out to be even worse than A. Then again, B may be as good or even better. Whom do you choose?

According to the Ellsberg paradox, we are far more likely to take our chances with the sure thing. But why? Economists historically explained this phenomenon by blaming our inherent fear of the unknown. Brain-imaging studies reveal that the amygdala (the region of the brain responsible for fear) is activated when it spots the mysterious jar B.[6] But newer research shows us that it's not so simple.

Let's bring out the jars again and add twenty economists and psychologists in lab coats, who are sitting in the room and watching you decide. Which jar do you choose? Adding observers to the room increases participants' aversion to the unknown. Fear of negative evaluation by others triggers a sense of vulnerability and sends people reaching for the known jar even more.[7]

But what happens if you remove the audience and thus the vulnerability? A team of researchers in the Netherlands designed a clever experiment to find out.[8] Participants selected a prize (one of two movies: *About a Boy* or *Catch Me If You Can*— both highly coveted in 2007), but they were instructed *not to tell anyone* which prize they wanted. Next, they placed an X sticker on one movie and an O on the other. Finally, they decided which deck of cards they wanted to play. One deck contained an equal number of X cards and O cards (like jar A), and the other deck contained an unknown mix of the two (like jar B). Once participants drew a card, they kept the movie corresponding with the sticker they placed on it. Only the participants knew whether they won or lost.

If our fear of the unknown depends on fear of negative evaluation, then removing all chances of being judged should reduce fear of the unknown. The researchers hypothesized that without fear of judgment, participants would select the mystery deck as often as the known probability deck. The findings surprised them. When participants were asked to tell observers which prize they wanted, they chose the mystery deck only 35 percent of the time (a typical pattern). But when they kept their prize preference private, they selected the mystery deck 67 percent of the time! With no fear of negative evaluation, we may actually prefer to take a chance and be surprised. This insight is important for those of us who are overwhelmed at the thought of embracing unpredictability. Is it the risk we fear, the vulnerability, or being judged? How many of our perfectly logical and reasonable choices are secretly influenced by fear?

So long as we fear vulnerability, we play it safe and stop ourselves from exploring. To practice reframing and get even more comfortable with vulnerability, we have to actively invite it in. There are countless ways to practice being open, but here are the three that work well as training wheels: own your mistakes, next notch, and ask for help. Think of this list as your personal vulnerability scavenger hunt. This week, search for opportunities to use each of these vulnerability-inducing techniques!

Own Your Mistakes

To test people's perception of mistakes, a team of social psychologists conducted an experiment.[9] They had participants listen to a recording of a student doing a mediocre job of answering questions on a quiz show. Then participants heard a crash and learned that he spilled his coffee. The researchers wanted to know how the coffee pratfall would affect people's perceptions of the student. They found that his already meager likeability scores dropped further after the clumsy accident.

When the researchers played a different recording—this time of an impressive student getting nearly every question right—the coffee spill *increased* his likeability. The screwup made him vulnerable, which humanized him and created connection. Making mistakes on top of mistakes doesn't earn us bonus points. But if we're skilled and competent, a few small fumbles can actually bolster our image and strengthen our relationships.

But there's something even more important than the mistakes themselves. What truly matters is how we handle them. Do we protect ourselves by hiding them or blaming them on something (or someone) else? Or do we stay open to surprise *and* own our mistakes, inviting in the unpredictable consequences?

Imagine that the CEO of a large company walks into a boardroom. Conversations fade. Papers stop rustling. Everyone turns to look at her. She clears her throat and says, "I was wrong." Chances are that in this moment she feels small and frightened. Her body doesn't know that she's a CEO. It only knows that she's human. When humans are ashamed, they want to hide under things. CEOs aren't supposed to hide under things, so she just stands there. What she doesn't realize is that on the other side of the table, her employees aren't condemning her for her mistake. They are admiring her for having the guts to own it. As Brené Brown puts it, "Vulnerability is courage in you and weakness in me."[10] The irony of vulnerability is that it often makes us feel small but look big.

Trendwatching.com points out a similar phenomenon with companies.[11] They coined the term *flawsome* to describe brands that admit their mistakes without explaining them away (for example, when Domino's publicly apologized for delivering very messy pizzas). The Trendwatching researchers argue that consumers don't love these vulnerable brands despite their mistakes but because of how they handle them. They write, "Human nature dictates that people have a hard time genuinely connecting with, being close to, or really trusting other humans who (pretend to) have no weaknesses, flaws, or mistakes."

Mistakes and flaws can trigger shame. We cope with shame by keeping it to ourselves. In fact, we share experiences of shame in less detail and with fewer people than all other emotional experiences.[12] The paradox is that talking about our shame is exactly what we need to move past it. Owning our mistakes relieves us of shame, earns trust, and inspires others to be open too.

Owning your mistakes is one of the most effective ways to invite vulnerability and get comfier with it. Pick just one tiny mistake or insecurity you have and tell people about it. Pay attention to how it feels, how it impacts others, and how it changes your relationships. Did you bond as a result? Did you give people the courage to share their own flaws with you? Did you feel just the teensiest bit better? If the experiment goes well, keep up the good work. The world can use more flawsome people.

Next Notch

We love this next exercise so much that we use it every day to push the boundaries of our vulnerability. Our rule is to reveal just one notch more than we are comfortable revealing in every interaction. We call it next notching. We're not talking about venting all of our hopes and fears in the middle of a meeting with a client but sharing a tiny bit more of ourselves than it feels safe to do. If there is a little part of us that wants to hide under the table, that's the little part that's going to have to stand under the spotlight.

Sometimes the next notch takes the form of admitting a weakness, sometimes a strength, often a personal story, and occasionally an attempted joke. Any genuine expression of who we really are can do the trick. For example, while writing this chapter, Tania scarfed down an entire bag of baby carrots, a bar of chocolate, a plate of cold fries, and all of her husband's cookies. She's not proud to admit it, but now you know (and so does he).

We can next notch through what we say, what we wear, and even what we show on our faces. In her research, LeeAnn found that we rate people with facial vulnerability (that is, facial expressions that are easy to read) as more likeable than people whose emotions are veiled. The better we can read people, the closer to them we feel.[13]

Next notching works on a personal level and, as Zappos illustrates, even on an organizational level. Unlike most corporate call centers, Zappos doesn't use scripts. Instead, phone reps listen and connect with their customers. They respond spontaneously and genuinely, like real human beings. This means no fake sympathy statements (*I sure am sorry to hear that, ma'am.*) and plenty of delightful tangents. Zappos also encourages next notching internally by promoting "a little bit of weirdness" as one of its core values. Weirdness can take many forms from flinging finger rockets across the room to sharing an Angry Birds cake when the atmosphere gets a little too serious. According to Zappos culture evangelist Donavon Roberson, encouraging employees to show what makes them weird allows them to feel accepted. Acceptance breeds trust and trust builds loyalty, creativity, and productivity.

The best thing about next notching is that it inspires others to lower their guard and become more vulnerable too, launching one of the world's loveliest virtuous cycles. To try this exercise, pay close attention to the words and expressions you hold back. Don't force them out at first. Just spend some time noticing. Once you're familiar with your own braking mechanism, ease off the brake a bit, take your vulnerability up a notch and allow yourself to be surprised by what happens.

Ask for Help

Musician Amanda Palmer used the crowd-funding site Kickstarter with the hope of raising $100,000 to produce a new album without a major record label. Instead she raised almost $1.2 million from her fans. Throughout her career she has also leaned on her social network for everything from a couch to crash on to restaurant recommendations.

Amanda works hard to stay vulnerable with her fans. She releases her music before it's finished so that she can complete it with her audience. She shares her hopes and fears on her blog. And she even weaves vulnerability stunts into her performances (like the time she wore a dress made out of balloons and invited fans to pop the dress until she stood naked before them). But the most transformative act of vulnerability Amanda practices is asking for help.

Again and again, Amanda has found that asking for help makes her feel vulnerable (people can always surprise us by saying no), but that very vulnerability is what inspires people to help. It's almost as though we have a built-in instinct to catch people when they fall. Helping isn't just natural, it's enjoyable. When we help others, our brains react with a distinct pattern of pleasure known as "helper's high."[14]

And yet, many of us go to incredible lengths to avoid asking for help. (You know who you are.) So our mission for you is this: Ask for help more often. We know you can do it on your own. Really. But getting help lets you practice vulnerability while connecting with others, delighting the helper, and maybe even making your life a little easier.

··· CHEAT SHEET ···

THE BITE-SIZE VERSION

Reframe vulnerability as openness rather than weakness. When we let ourselves be vulnerable, we experience life more fully and build deeper connections. Cool is the enemy of growth. Protection is the enemy of connection. Distance is the enemy of influence.

TOOLS

- **Own your mistakes:** invite connection by talking about your mistakes and weaknesses (without subtly blaming them on someone or something else).
- **Next notch:** reveal just one notch more than you feel comfortable revealing.
- **Ask for help:** find small ways to ask people to lend you a hand.

EXERCISE YOUR SURPRISE MUSCLE

You're at a gathering with people you don't know. The atmosphere is stiff. Before calling it a night, give these folks one more shot. Reframe vulnerability as openness and come up with ways to build connections with the guests.

. . . .

Chapter Five

Practice Skillful Not-Knowing

When Kristen Powers was eleven years old, her father took her and her brother to Disney World. They shrieked through Splash Mountain. Snapped enough family photos to make a stop-motion video. And plopped into the car for the ride home still covered in a thin coat of cotton candy. That's when he told them: "Your mother has Huntington's disease."

Kristen had long suspected that something was wrong with her mother. She had always been clumsy. But in the past couple of years, Nicole Powers wasn't just dropping things, she was tripping and falling—once breaking her nose. She began to look drunk when she walked. When she took the kids to the movies, she repeatedly kicked the seat in front of her, mortifying Kristen and her brother.

Huntington's disease is a neuropsychiatric disorder described as a combination of Parkinson's disease, Alzheimer's disease, bipolar disorder, and Lou Gehrig's disease. That's right.

All of those. Symptoms generally appear between the ages of thirty-five and forty-five: cognitive decline, fatigue, loss of motor control, and unpredictable changes in mood. Within a few years of their first signs of decline, Huntington's patients can no longer care for themselves and rapidly, horrifyingly degenerate. Soon after Kristen found out about her mother's diagnosis, she got an even bigger surprise: There was a 50 percent chance she had it too. Genetic tests allow children of Huntington's patients to find out whether they are destined for the same fate, but they have to wait until their eighteenth birthdays to get tested.

For Kristen, the experience of not knowing colored everything in her life. Between the day she decided to get tested and the day she found out her status, all she could do was worry and wait. Her brain was forced into the Find Phase of the Surprise Sequence for *seven years*.

As our world changes more rapidly, all of our lives are becoming infused with the tension of the unknown. We interviewed Kristen to learn more about how to adapt to this tension and embrace unpredictability. Resilience is the first step, reframing and inviting in vulnerability come next, but can we also become *skilled at not-knowing*? There are plenty of courses and institutions dedicated to skillful knowledge. But what about mastery of uncertainty and ambiguity? How can we get good at accepting and navigating these states of being? We thought if anyone had this unique skill set, it had to be Kristen.

"The suspense was literally going to make me throw up or pass out," she said about the day her results finally came in. Kristen's genetic counselor got right to the point: "I have good news for you today. You tested negative." Relief. Joy. Gratitude.

Kristen spent the rest of the day as the messenger of her life's two most precious words: *good news*. But by the next day, a surprising new feeling settled in: "Suddenly the possibilities were endless," said Kristen. "I was like, oh my God, is this how normal people feel?"

That's the question we'll investigate in this chapter. How do we normal people feel about the endless unknowns in our lives? And how can we practice skillful not-knowing so that unpredictability doesn't cripple us with anxiety or prevent us from exploring the surprises in life? Kristen spent her adolescence wondering which of her *two* possible futures would be her reality. But a negative diagnosis (no Huntington's) meant a future of not just two but *infinite* unknowns. Though it is rarely as salient to us as it was to Kristen, this limitless, unimaginable future, full of uncertainty and ambiguity—this giant question mark waiting to take us by surprise—is the reality that most of us have the privilege and pain of facing.

UNCERTAINTY

We process uncertainty much like we process surprise. The P300 wave that hijacks our mental resources when we're surprised has a part-time job in the uncertainty department.[1] When we aren't sure what to expect, the P300 hoards a hefty chunk of our attention so that we are better prepared for surprise when it happens. Just like surprise, the tension of uncertainty evolved to keep us far from danger and close to opportunity.

Our ancestors likely handled uncertainty in two ways: avoiding uncertainty and approaching certainty (similar to their prehistoric cousins, flight and fight). The avoid response entailed retreating to a comfort zone (staying clear of dark caves and weird new berries). The approach response consisted of exploring the unknown (those very same dark caves and weird smelling berries).

Both evolutionary strategies were surprise busters. The avoid response kept us away from anything that might surprise us. The approach response pushed us to prevent surprise by predicting and controlling our environments. These days there are no saber-tooths hanging out in neighborhood caves, and our chances of being poisoned by mystery fruit at the supermarket are (we hope) slim, but our bodies still try to eliminate the possibility of surprise. The trouble is that this instinct is no longer adaptive.

Thanks to our desire to avoid uncertainty and prevent bad surprises many of us select the dull and demotivating sure thing (like dead-end jobs and relationships) over fulfilling but uncertainty-ridden options (like following our dreams). Avoidance in response to uncertainty is still useful in truly dangerous situations, but in most instances, doing nothing is not a good option. Relationships, innovation, success, and fulfillment all come to those willing to take a risk and face surprise.

Tackling uncertainty head-on through the approach response isn't the more adaptive alternative either. Taking action too quickly or thoughtlessly can lead to dangerous mistakes or just plain lousy decisions. The approach response also leads to a prediction paradox. In negative situations (such as having to fire an employee), we try to regain certainty by predicting the future. In other words, we ruminate. In so doing we trigger anxiety. And when we try to predict positive events (for example, how much of a bonus we'll get), we invite disappointment and limit the pleasure we would have experienced from the event if we allowed it to surprise us.[2] If you've ever looked through photos of your destination long before your vacation then found yourself underwhelmed while actually there, you've fallen victim to the prediction paradox. Or, as we like to say, you've Googled away delight.

We avoid uncertainty and approach certainty in an effort to prevent surprise and protect ourselves, but we wind up shooting ourselves in the foot. How do we turn the proverbial pistol in another direction and become skillful not-knowers?

THE MIDDLE WAY

Filmmaker Roko Belic wanted to uncover the secret to happiness, so he traveled to fourteen countries and interviewed hundreds of people to gain a deeper understanding of this timelessly coveted and elusive emotion. (You can watch the highlights of his adventure in the documentary *Happy*.) One of the things Roko noticed along the way was that some cultures seemed happier than others. How did the happiest cultures differ? In part it was their ability to accept uncertainty. This mind-set alone allowed them to embrace unpredictability and stay open to surprise.

In an interview that made *us* very happy, Roko spoke about his experience with the San Bushmen of Namibia who still live in a hunter-gatherer society: "The belief they hold is that if you go hunting for gazelle but capture a porcupine instead, that's okay too. Hunting is inherently spontaneous and unpredictable. If you try to control it too much and avoid all surprises, you'll miss out on opportunities. Hunting is the core of San existence, so this philosophy is central to their lives."

The San have no electricity, indoor plumbing, or running water. Every year the possibility of drought threatens their survival (not to mention the scorpions and poisonous snakes). And yet, if you hang out with the San, you'll notice that a huge chunk of their time is spent talking, laughing, dancing, and singing together. Happiness for the San does not depend on knowing what the future will bring. Some might even say that their happiness depends on *not* knowing what the future will bring and simply enjoying the possibilities.

There have been so many technological and scientific developments in our modern world that it may seem strange to point to a population whose culture looks as though it got trapped in a time warp. Fifty years ago, we would have agreed with you, but today—just as for the San—surprise is once again an everyday feature of our ecosystem. In this respect, we have a lot more in common with our hunter-gatherer ancestors than our grandparents did.

So how are the San (and those who share their philosophy) different from the average knowledge-needy human? We think the most valuable lesson from their perspective is their ability to follow the Middle Way.

The Middle Way lies between our desire to avoid uncertainty and approach certainty. It is the perfect balance on the Surprise Seesaw. It means accepting that surprises will happen without trying to avoid them or predict them. Accepting surprise is a deceptively simple kernel of wisdom, and it is valuable on its own, but if you're ready to graduate to the next level, we'll show you some more tools for skillful not-knowing and taking action from the middle. Over the years, we've worked with some of the world's most revolutionary companies and individuals, and we've gotten to use these tools with them in a wide range of contexts. In other words, even if you don't plan on hunting gazelle, you'll likely find the following tools helpful: call it an experiment, scenario plan, and improvise.

Call It an Experiment

Individuals and organizations that make great decisions in the midst of uncertainty think differently from traditional decision makers. Traditional decision making is based on the premise that you have to lock yourself in a room with all the facts (preferably printed in tiny font on heavy stacks of paper), spend the night weighing all your options, then make one final decision and commit to it. This philosophy is based on the belief that certainty is possible.

Modern-day decision makers don't even think of themselves as making decisions. They call it an experiment. Ingrid Fetell, senior design researcher at the legendary design firm IDEO told us, "If you feel like you have to make one final decision, your impulse will be to collect every bit of relevant information. In the past maybe it was possible to feel like you collected everything, but today your search would be endless. There is too much information out there. So instead, you have to focus on figuring things out one small experiment at a time."

When we think of our decisions as experiments, we remember that uncertainty is normal and surprises will always happen. From this perspective, there is no such thing as the right decision—instead, the best decision is one that can be tested, bent, curved, and ultimately changed. To launch some experiments of your own, the next time you have a decision to make, form a hypothesis instead. Test the hypothesis. Collect the data. Then confirm or revise your hypothesis. You don't even need a lab coat.

Scenario Plan

Future 1: Go Broke. If you quit your job and start a company, you might burn through your savings in six months and be forced to move in with your mom.

Future 2: Strike Gold. Investors might instantly see the value in your idea and fork over millions of dollars.

Future 3: Uphill Battle. You may find enough clients to cover your minimal expenses but spend many years developing a business that will earn you a decent salary.

These three versions of the future are a brief demonstration of scenario planning, another decision-making model from the Middle Way. This tool was devised to withstand uncertainty and the surprises that follow. To apply scenario planning to your own work or personal life, concoct a few very different stories of the future based on the information you already have. Should you quit your job and start a company? Should you buy a car?

Should you hire an assistant? Get together with an imaginative and diverse group of daydreamers and write out all the potential futures you can envision. The point isn't to predict what will happen (though you might have your fingers crossed for Future 2) but to explore the many possibilities.

Once you've invented your scenarios, your goal is to devise a decision that can flex to fit any one of your possible futures. For example, if you quit your job but can't find a client by the time rent is due, how will you handle the situation? Not only will scenario planning prepare you for an array of outcomes and prevent you from fixating on a single vision of the future, it can also quiet the chattering part of your brain obsessed with bringing the Find Phase to a close.

When we asked Kristen Powers which strategy best helped her cope with the uncertainty of Huntington's, she described scenario planning even though she had never heard the term. Kristen told us: "I kind of divided my future life into two: a positive diagnosis future and a negative diagnosis future. Like if I had Huntington's disease, I would take a year off before starting college and visit all seven continents. If I didn't have Huntington's, I'd start college right away, and I'd still travel, but Antarctica could probably wait." Whatever happened, she knew she had a plan. This prep work allowed her brain to stop predicting the future and savor the present.

Improvise

It's just another night at the PIT (the Peoples Improv Theater in New York), but the setting has all the markings of an archetypical nightmare: You're on stage, staring at an audience that's staring back at you. You have no idea what your co-stars or you will say next. Few can stomach this challenge. And yet, improvisational theater (improv) is growing in popularity. Perhaps because the improv stage is looking a lot like our everyday lives.

Improvising is a fascinating art form because the best improvisers are the most open to surprise. An improviser's job is to not know. The audience and the actors all want to be surprised. The more surprised the actors, the more delighted the audience. Performers who follow a script of any kind quickly lose their audience's interest.

How can we all get better at improvising offstage? We spoke with Ali Farahnakian and Dion Flynn to find out. Ali opened the PIT after being a founding member of the Upright Citizens Brigade, a performer at Chicago's the Second City, and a writer for *Saturday Night Live*. Dion is a regular on *The Tonight Show* with Jimmy Fallon and a longtime improv performer and instructor.

They agreed that the most important rule in improv is listening to your scene partners rather than thinking about yourself. Listen, stay curious, and jump in to advance the story—even if you're not quite sure where to take it. The same advice applies offstage. In times of uncertainty, turning our attention to others allows us to move more swiftly and make better choices. It also allows us to help others look good, which builds trust and community.

Improvising well also means having no attachment to outcome. "All suffering comes from attachment," says Ali. "You can't get attached to the way things will turn out in a scene, and you can't get attached to the way things turn out in life." When improv performers decide where they want the scene to go, the performance immediately loses its sizzle. The most exciting performers trust that they'll find themselves someplace better than they imagined, which is precisely how they get there. To improvise, we have to stay with the moment we're in instead of chasing a moment we want. When we let go of our attachments, surprise becomes the messenger of opportunity instead of a rain cloud over our perfectly planned parade. To improvise more in your life, notice interactions that seem stiff or scripted. Spot times when you are overly attached to an outcome or slamming down on metaphorical brakes. Allow yourself to change direction and stay curious about where you'll wind up. Eventually, you'll get comfortable enough to roll down your windows and enjoy the ride.

Experimenting, scenario planning, and improvising don't avoid uncertainty or approach certainty. They accept surprise and move with it. But what if your problem isn't uncertainty but a different kind of not-knowing? Uncertainty arises from insufficient information. Ambiguity is vagueness and confusion brought on by *too much* information. Let's take a deeper look at the latter.

AMBIGUITY

Spend a moment gazing at the image on the next page. It is ambiguous. There are at least two ways to view it, but the first image you spot is the only one you'll see without extra cognitive huffing and puffing. Sometimes this type of image is called an optical illusion, though strictly speaking, there's no trick to it.

It's simply two different things coexisting in one package. The challenge of ambiguity also applies to ideas. As in the case of uncertainty, we've evolved with two ways to cope with ambiguity: avoidance and approach. Avoidance in the face of ambiguity works like avoidance in response to uncertainty. When something is too complex, confusing, or different from our beliefs, we simply leave it alone.

The other response is approaching certainty, a tactic more commonly known as "making up our minds" or "jumping to conclusions." We often crave the feeling of knowing so much that we erect a psychological fortress around our schemata to prevent them from shifting. We keep the surprise out. This response is innate but also heavily reinforced by society.

In most countries, schools are built to teach kids the "right" answers. If you've ever taken a multiple-choice exam, you know the dangers of making an accidental pencil mark outside the correct circle. In this world, there is only A, B, C, D, and maybe E, and absolutely nothing in between. In schools around the world, learning is synonymous with reciting information. Within this paradigm there is no such thing as the gray area (not even partial credit). With the best intentions, we reinforce knowing and certainty so consistently that periods of ambiguity look like a giant F on the report cards of our lives. We become skilled knowers and incompetent not-knowers. While this practice may have been aligned with a slow, factory-dominated society, it is no longer adaptive in our fast-paced, idea-driven world.

Consider also how most cultures treat the hesitant or, worse still, vacillating individual. Just a quick dip into an English thesaurus reveals that we have a plethora of words describing individuals who change their minds easily—none of them particularly positive. We have fickle, wavering, capricious, inconsistent, indecisive, irresolute, faltering, unsteady, flighty, volatile, frivolous, lubricious, fitful, erratic, faithless, flip-flopping, wishy-washy, double-crossing, and even yo-yo.

Now take a look at the antonyms list: certain, steady, stable, reliable, consistent, constant, steadfast, faithful, resolute, unyielding, firm, solid, dependable, loyal, trusty, and a rock. The second list brings to mind a powerful oak—its rich leaves flooded with sunshine. The first list leads us to imagine a spineless creature, scuttling into some dank cavity in the sidewalk. *Resolute* sounds honorable; *flip-flopping* sounds weak. It's not just a matter of what made its way into a dictionary; as linguists will tell you, our words reveal our values.

Nowhere is the deep-seated value of knowing as evident as in the realm of politics. Voters and newspapers urge candidates to be open-minded and consider many sides when making a decision. In reality, politicians risk crippling their careers if they change their minds (thereby revealing that they've experienced a schema shift). During the 2004 U.S. presidential election, John Kerry learned this lesson the hard way when he changed his stance on contributing funds to the war in Iraq and Afghanistan. The decision earned him the nickname Flip-Flop Kerry and, analysts suspect, may have cost him the job. To this day, you can still purchase a pair of John Kerry flip-flop sandals.

We battle to change other people's minds and then we wonder why it never seems to work. Not only do we have rigid schemata and social norms to contend with, there's also the matter of the backfire effect: the harder we try to change people's minds, the more firmly they stand by their beliefs.[3] Threatened schemata are like frightened hedgehogs, curling up into spiky little balls and protecting themselves from predators (that is, surprises that may lead them to shift). Yet some of us handle ambiguity differently.

GOT FLEX?

Researchers at the Berlin Wisdom Project went around the city in search of its wisest citizens.[4] They asked the individuals who were nominated by their communities a series of questions. Here's one: "A fifteen-year-old girl approaches you for advice. She wants to drop out of school, marry her boyfriend, and have a baby. What do you tell her?"

The individuals in the control group (the average folks) were decisive and impassioned. Their answers were usually along the lines of "Are you kidding me? No way in hell should you get married at fifteen!" (albeit in German). The wise people behaved differently. They took time to think. Even then, they often chose not to respond at all. They explained that they didn't want to jump to conclusions without learning the whole story. They accepted the tension of ambiguity and preferred it to a rash reply. These were skilled not-knowers.

This attitude stems straight from the Middle Way. It is neither avoidance nor the pursuit of certainty. Psychologists call the ability to suspend judgment and hold opposing views in one's mind tolerance for ambiguity. We like to call it flexing—allowing a constant shifting and stretching to happen to our schemata. Individuals with flex are open to surprise because they can maintain doubt for days, months, and even lifetimes. They can let their opinions adapt to new information while leaving enough wiggle room to revise them once again.

Paul Saffo, managing director of foresight at Discern Analytics puts it this way: In times of ambiguity, it is best to have "strong opinions, weakly held."[5] We like this phrasing because it suggests that flexing doesn't have to mean floating about, believing in nothing (though Socrates seemed to pull that off quite well). For most of us, it means allowing our schemata to shift when we're surprised. In other words, allowing our beliefs to change.

Tolerance for ambiguity is correlated with positive risk-taking and life satisfaction.[6] Some of us naturally maintain flex throughout our lives, but we can all learn to flex more. We'd like to show you two of our favorite tools for developing more flex (and thus being more open to surprise): Get to the pot of gold on the other side of awkward and engage in reverse debates.

Get to the Pot of Gold on the Other Side of Awkward

Although some of the ambiguous situations that trigger our approach and avoid reactions have truly dangerous consequences, most of them are just plain awkward. We feel awkward when we aren't sure what to do or how to act (*Which one is the salad fork, again?*), and the most painful ambiguous situations are the kinds that involve other people.

As our world becomes more complex and culturally diverse, we can look forward to even more awkward opportunities. To adapt to ambiguity and build flex, practice getting to the pot of gold on the other side of awkward on a regular basis. Instead of avoiding awkward moments, start collecting them. (We promise that an awkwardness collection can beat out even the most impressive stamp collection.) Identify the value that lies just beyond the awkwardness and wade smack into the middle of the situation. Know that it usually gets worse before it gets better. But the end result is worth it.

To get to the pot of gold on the other side of awkward more often, seek out situations that feel uncomfortable. Start small with mini awkward missions like chatting with a stranger on an elevator or putting together a piece of furniture without instructions. Observe how the following three moments feel: just before you step into it, the peak of awkwardness, and the point at which you reach the gold (bonding, pride, learning, etc.). Awkwardness is your body's way of telling you that you are learning and changing. Remind yourself that if you back away from awkward, you back away from growth. The good news is, the more often you make the trip across awkwardness, the easier future trips become. And if nothing else, you'll walk away with a great story for your collection.

Engage in Reverse Debates

If you decide to develop flex by speaking to strangers, we recommend you make those strangers as different from you as possible. In our interviews with individuals who have changed their minds on major topics such as gun control and religion, we found that exposure to opposing views had an impact on their thinking—but only if it wasn't presented in the form of a debate. Remember the backfire effect? Few of us change our minds when someone is pressuring us. Pressure to change typically makes us protect our schemata and stay exactly as we are.

Surveys of popular opinion on gay marriage found that one in three people who changed their minds to support gay marriage did so because they met someone gay.[7] The same phenomenon plays out with racial, ethnic, gender, age, and religious prejudices. When we keep a distance from opposing views, we subject ourselves to a bias called out-group homogeneity: the belief that people in our in-group (those who share our beliefs and characteristics) are all unique, but "they" or "the others" are all the same. Why do we have this bias? Our brains prefer to simplify information so that it's easier to digest. Simple feels nice. It makes life less confusing. But it also prevents us from growing, changing, and connecting to people who don't share our norms. When we integrate "us" with "them" we experience intense ambiguity but we also build flex, which lets us adapt to surprising new information.

If you don't have easy access to diverse individuals in person, take advantage of the whole wide world online, in books, and in newspapers. As an experiment in developing flex, select an opinion that feels certain to you. Spend at least one week immersing yourself in the opposing view. Instead of noticing how this view differs from yours, engage in a reverse debate: spot all the little ways in which your worldview is similar to the other side. In what ways do you agree with them?

If all else fails, spend some time exploring how social norms have changed over time. Just in the past fifty years in the United States, we've changed our minds about racial segregation, gay rights, women in the workplace, animal rights, and recycling. When people look back on us in fifty more years, which of our "obviously correct" beliefs will look as crazy to them then as "separate but equal" looks to us today?

If your first attempts at intentional not-knowing don't go as well as you like, keep it up. Just the fact that you are reading this book tells us that you are already more comfortable with the unknown than the typical person. You've come a long way, and it is a challenging road for all of us (even the really wise folks). We've spent our entire lives learning to know. As a society, we are just taking baby steps when it comes to being good at not-knowing.

THE BITE-SIZE VERSION

We feel uncertain when we can't predict what will happen. We experience ambiguity when there are too many options. Our brains are wired to eliminate both types of unknowns. We avoid them or we rush to reach a sense of certainty. Neither approach is adaptive. Instead of following our instincts, we can become skilled at not-knowing. Take action from the Middle Way and build your cognitive flex.

TOOLS

- **Call it an experiment:** making a final decision can feel paralyzing. Instead, call your decisions experiments and repeat them until you like the result.
- **Scenario plan:** devise several stories of possible futures and create a plan that is flexible enough to fit any of them.
- **Improvise:** focus on others instead of on yourself and don't be attached to outcome.
- **Get to the pot of gold on the other side of awkward:** collect awkwardness the way you would collect stamps. Remind yourself that you have to wade through awkwardness to reach connection, fulfillment, and growth.
- **Engage in reverse debates:** select views that seem very different from yours and spot all the ways in which they are actually similar to what you believe.

EXERCISE YOUR SURPRISE MUSCLE

You're starting a project in an unfamiliar field. You're feeling insecure, and it doesn't help that some people in your company are excited about the project while others say it's bound to fail. You find yourself awake at night. What can you do to embrace the unpredictability?

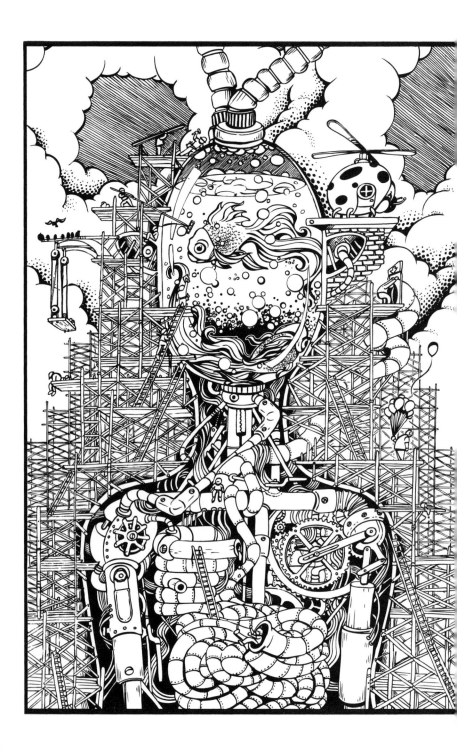

PART THREE

Engineer the UNEXPECTED

*I've learned that you shouldn't go
through life with
a catcher's mitt on both hands;
you need to be able to throw something back.*

—MAYA ANGELOU

By now you have a richer understanding of how surprise can trap us in our comfort zones and rush us into certainty. You've also picked up tools to embrace the unpredictable so that it transforms from an enemy into an ally. You're building greater resilience, a new perspective on vulnerability, and sharper skills for handling uncertainty and ambiguity. We hope you also have more insight into the feelings and behaviors of those around you so that you can help them welcome the unpredictable too. Embracing surprise allows us to become explorers, and there is so much in this life to explore.

But letting surprise in isn't enough. We have to let surprise *out* too. Each of us has the capacity and maybe even the responsibility to surprise the world. We are infinitely capable of the unexpected. It is a crying shame to live life as though it came with an instruction manual.

This section of the book is an ode to living life all the way. It is about engineering the unexpected rather than simply accepting it. Because you picked up this book, we already know that you get it. You're probably already surprising the people around you. Our goal is to help you get even better at it. There are infinite ways to create surprise. You can engineer the unexpected by weaving more surprise into your gifts, stories, compliments, inventions, events, presentations, products, classes, services, meals, outfits, and conversations. The scope of the surprises doesn't matter. Even the smallest surprise can make a big impact. Actually, the smallest surprises often matter most. By engineering the unexpected you can:

- Transform an unpleasant task into a fun activity.
- Make a gathering more memorable.
- Turn small talk into an adventure.
- Get people to smile more.
- Tell a story in a way that fascinates listeners.
- Bring a new idea to life.

In short, by engineering the unexpected, you will turn ordinary into extraordinary. Surprise-making might already come naturally to you, but think of this section of the book as your school of advanced surprise engineering. We want to amplify your raw surprise-making power by introducing you to the concept of skillful surprise. When most people plot a surprise, they use it like a blunt instrument. You are about to discover how to use it like a scalpel. Becoming a surprise engineer is a bit like that scene in *The Matrix* when Neo can suddenly dodge bullets because time seems to slow down. That's what happens when you understand something deeply (well, sort of). Instead of leaving you to juggle infinite possibilities, we'll arm you with tools to create surprise strategically. Not only will you brighten people's days but you'll also get to relish the joy and surprise of seeing their reactions.

When should you use these tools? Think back to the Surprise Sequence. What are your best opportunities to get people to stop, plug into the moment, get curious, shift their perspectives, and talk to others about their experiences? What ordinary, taken-for-granted items, events, and interactions can you infuse with surprise to make them memorable? Where have you spotted low or no expectations? What people, groups, places, and routines could benefit from some disruption and emotional intensification? What ordinary aspects of life can you make extraordinary?

Is surprisifying the world your responsibility? Absolutely. Without you, things will go on just as they are. Without you, people will go to bed with no memory of their day (because nothing particularly interesting happened). They'll grow up and forget to be amazed. They'll let years pass without learning anything new. Worst of all, they'll forget that someone cares deeply about them and believes they're worthy of special attention—that they are important enough for someone to surprise them.

We'll begin this section of the book by exploring how you can get even more creative to devise new surprise ideas. We'll discuss how you can wield attention so that your surprises make the biggest impact. Then you'll be ready for two advanced engineering skills that will take your surprises to the next level: designing delight and making experiences. The best part is that no one knows where this training will take you. Not even you.

. . . . . .

Get Creative

It's 6:50 p.m. on a frigid Thursday in New York City. So cold that everyone walks around silent because opening your mouth means inviting in a biting gust of wind. We enter the industrial-looking elevator of Quirky headquarters, half-expecting to find the giant office (a renovated storage facility) to be deserted. The building is housed so far from the center of the city that trains don't run there. The lure of a toasty apartment is almost irresistible. But when the elevator doors open, we see that the space is packed. There are only two empty seats (right behind a column), so we grab them.

At 7 p.m. sharp, Quirky's founder, Ben Kaufman, starts the show. What we're watching, or rather participating in, is a weekly event called Eval. It's free and open to the public. Aspiring innovators submit their invention ideas through the site (more than 4,000 every week), and over 600,000 users vote for the best ones. Approximately twelve make it to Eval. Here the community votes for its favorites. Once an idea is chosen, Quirky engineers build it and put it on the market.

Eval is fast-paced, spirited, and everyone is drinking beer. Ideas flash on the screen. The audience murmurs, laughs, oohs, and boos. If an idea is particularly titillating, we become a sea of Duh Faces, stunned into silence by the surprise. A computer monitor that adjusts to your vision. A fake hand to sooth your crying baby. Solar-powered battery chargers. A smartphone-operated pet feeder. A self-inflating fort. Aside from the inventions themselves, two questions strike us as particularly fascinating:

> Why is Quirky so popular?
>
> How do people come up with all of these creative and surprising ideas?

Creativity means making something new or finding a new way to look at something old. If you are going to be engineering the unexpected, you're going to have to get creative. In fact, as we'll discuss in this chapter, creativity is becoming vital for all of us. We'll talk about the growing importance of creativity in our world. Then we'll spend the rest of this chapter on what it takes to keep up with Quirky's contributors and devise unexpected new ideas.

CREATIVITY GOES MAINSTREAM

Not long ago, creativity was the domain of people with unusual haircuts. You could draw a clear, nonsquiggly line between the creatives and the professionals. A few odd birds actually got paid to come up with ideas, but most people did "practical" work. These days, things are different. Creativity has gone mainstream. We've seen an explosion of surprising new creations through sites like Quirky, Etsy, YouTube, and Kickstarter. And even the most practical professional today has to be creative. How come?

As we discussed in Chapter 2, our speed of communication is increasing exponentially. If you get annoyed when someone doesn't respond to your email within eight hours, imagine what it was like to wait for a carrier pigeon. Quicker communication means quicker creation and spread of ideas. At the same time, the cost of making just about anything (from websites to physical objects) is plummeting. Routine tasks are outsourced to computers, freeing us up for even more creative thinking. The barriers to creativity are dropping and creative competition is heating up. As Thomas Wedell-Wedellsborg, author of *Innovation as Usual*, said to us, "Suddenly, we're competing with two hundred guys in two hundred other garages."

Even if we don't want to bring something new into existence, we have no choice but to get creative. We have to engineer surprise to adapt to all the surprises popping up around us. Creativity isn't just a matter of producing new gadgets; it's also what allows us to respond to unexpected disruptions in technology, science, government, and even our personal lives. In this sense, creativity isn't a perk of living in the modern world—it's a core requirement. That makes it an incredibly exciting time to be a human. Not only do we get to be surprised by our world, we also get to surprise it right back.

CREATIVITY TOOLS

In this chapter we'll introduce you to four tools that will help you generate ideas to transform the ordinary into the extraordinary (whether you want to come up with an unexpected product or an unexpected gift): get to curious, live in the fog, practice idea mixology, and iterate. As you encounter each tool, apply it to a specific context (*How can I surprise my girlfriend?*) and to life in general (*Where else can I turn up the vibrancy dial by engineering the unexpected?*).

Get to Curious

Opportunities to engineer the unexpected are sitting right in front of us, twiddling their thumbs until we notice them. The heart of creativity is shifting our perception to spot these opportunities. But that's easier said than done. Consider a story that Thomas Wedell-Wedellsborg shared with us about creativity in the world of suitcases.

The suitcase had been around for ages in the form of a big rectangle with a handle. It wasn't until 1970 that someone thought to put wheels on it.[1] The first rolling suitcases were an improvement, but they were hard to maneuver. And they tipped over a lot. They were identical to the old suitcases, only with four wheels and a leash to drag it with. An entire seventeen years passed before someone realized you could turn the suitcase on its side and add a telescoping handle, saving billions of people from frustration and back pain. This idea seems obvious in retrospect, but the rigid schemata in people's minds made creative suitcase alternatives invisible. What other "obvious" opportunities to engineer the unexpected are we overlooking? How can our conversations, products, services, events, and dinners be more surprising?

Our favorite creativity tool for spotting surprise opportunities is getting to curious. Think of it as hacking into the Surprise Sequence. Surprise triggers curiosity, and curiosity triggers surprise. Instead of waiting for the Freeze Phase, we can train ourselves to start at the Find Phase. To get to curious, think of "curious" as a place you go rather than a feeling you have. Whenever you are stuck, frustrated, or uninspired, imagine stepping into an elevator that takes you to the curious floor. Ding! The doors open, and suddenly everything is fascinating.

For an express pass to curious, play Twenty Questions, a game we use with students at LifeLabs New York. Pick a familiar object, like a pencil, and come up with twenty questions about it. Why is it this color? Who made it? What tree did it come from? How much does it weigh? Who can I poke with it? How else can I use it? In LifeLabs New York creativity classes, we notice that people usually get stuck around question nine. If they keep trying, their curiosity kicks in and the really interesting questions surface. (Pro tip: The best questions almost always start with *why*.) You can select any object to play this game or you can play it with the subject for which you need ideas. If no ideas surface right away, don't despair. Once you've gotten to curious, a part of you will stay there until you've come to a conclusion. You may even be surprised by a fully formed idea when you wake up the next morning. The curious part of your brain keeps working even as you sleep. And if no ideas come, read on.

Live in the Fog

When Spencer Silver created the product that we now know as the Post-it note, he was attempting to devise a super-strong adhesive.[2] He made the exact opposite by accident. Instead of treating the weak glue as a mistake, he got to curious and asked, "What is this thing?" and "How can it be useful?" When no one could figure out what to do with Spencer's flimsy glue, he didn't stop there. He stayed curious for five years.

Spencer talked about his odd invention with everyone who'd listen. Eventually, he bumped into his colleague Art Fry who suggested that the glue could tack notes to a page without ruining the paper. The idea stuck (get it?) and eventually made a fortune but only because Spencer never stopped wrestling with it. We like to think of this creativity tool as living in the fog, a term we learned from the design firm IDEO. "The fog" is where IDEOers spend most of their time.

Donald O. Hebb, one of the founders of neuropsychology, was the first scientist to speculate about what goes on within the fog.[3] He pointed out that insight—that glorious aha! moment that we associate with creativity—is just the visible tip of the creativity iceberg. First the brain arranges information (pulling in more and more of it from the world) and only then does it turn to the creative work of rearranging information. First Find, then Shift. We glorify the apple that fell on Newton's head, sparking the idea of gravity, but we usually ignore the fact that Newton wasn't just a random guy sitting under a tree. He was a scientist and a mathematician who had spent years wondering about the way the world works. He was a man who spent all of his time in the fog, and the apple just served to clear the mist.

As you may remember from Chapter 5, we generally deal with the fog of the unknown by avoiding it or pushing through it. But the most creative individuals live in it. Like the wise people of Berlin, when no answers come, they simply stay curious and wait. They stretch the Find Phase of the Surprise Sequence and live in the fog as long as they need to. Creative ideas greet them on the other side.

To use this tool you can simply reframe moments of frustration and confusion as the fog and recognize that the feeling is normal. Or you can go a step further and play in the fog intentionally. Begin with an open-ended question like, *What should my next blog post be about?* or *How can I grow my business?* Instead of reaching for an answer, follow the Middle Way and give yourself time to ponder. We recommend setting aside a week or longer. Don't come to any conclusions until your time is up.

While in the fog, collect your thoughts and observations in one reliable place. Gather newspaper clippings, words, clothing, images, or anything else that stirs you ever so slightly. Don't bother asking why this particular thing has gotten your attention. Just add it to your collection. Bring your question to mind every day without searching for answers. Review your collection every few days without searching for patterns. Most important, don't just sit there. Remember that Spencer didn't have his aha! moment about the Post-it note alone in his office. He spent five years going out and talking about it to new people. Which brings us to our next tool . . .

Practice Idea Mixology

The engineers of the Japanese railway system had a big problem. They designed one of the world's fastest trains, but it had a major flaw. Every time it passed through a tunnel, it emitted a deafening *boom* on its way out. They had to make the train quieter. But how? It just so happened that the project's chief engineer, Eiji Nakatsu, liked to watch birds.[4] While wrestling with the challenge of the loud train, he saw a kingfisher in action. The kingfisher bird plunges directly from air to water with almost no splash. Unlike the noisy train, the kingfisher is sleek and silent. Thanks to this tip from nature, Eiji changed the front of the train to model the kingfisher's beak. The result? A train that is significantly quieter, 10 percent faster, and uses 15 percent less electricity.

That's just one example of how surprising mixtures spark creativity. Making unexpected combinations or, as we like to say, practicing idea mixology, is how most new ideas are born. To practice idea mixology, you can visit a new place, read a book you expect to hate, or speak to someone whose views are radically different from yours. Even taking a walk outside (where new sensations and experiences await) increases creative output by 60 percent.[5]

To help mix things up online, computer scientist Steve Nelson built BananaSlug, a search engine that inserts something random into your query to dig up a result you'd never reach by following the path of good, clean logic. For example, if you enter the term *woodchuck*, BananaSlug might pair it with an emotion, color, or theme from Shakespeare. Steve calls it "serendipitous surfing." The result is almost always a surprise (and sometimes it's more helpful than Google). Steve told us, "To come up with a new idea you have to throw in surprise and knock the system off its equilibrium."

Idea mixology explains why most of us have our best ideas in the shower or in the middle of the grocery store instead of at work. If we're thinking about the same thing in the same way, our thoughts become surprise resistant, and we need something different to flex our schemata and spark insight. The longer we spend pondering down the same path, the more desperately we need a dose of surprise (and the less comfortable it is to let surprise in). Mixing routine with surprise creates an unbeatable creativity concoction. Rather than hoping to bump into surprise, the most creative individuals find a way to make idea mixology inevitable.

To get his employees mixing regularly at Pixar, its cofounder Steve Jobs had architects design the office for maximum collisions.[6] One of his ideas was even to have all of the bathrooms in the center of the building, forcing everyone to leave their departments and mingle in the middle. Quirky schedules a quarterly blackout for all employees, giving them paid time off and an absolutely no working rule so that they can go out into the world and do random things. Surprise Industries facilitates idea mixology by inviting people to step into unusual new experiences. And LifeLabs New York helps spark ideas by giving learners regular access to new concepts and skills through our labs.

Practicing idea mixology can also be as simple as subscribing to a random array of magazines (from *Cycle World* to *Cat Fancy*), attending competing events (from March for Life to the

Reproductive Rights Retreat), designating one day every month to have a new experience, or just spending time outside (where small surprises like flowers, leaves, and apples are likely to fall on your head). You can use idea mixology as a tool when you're stumped and need a new perspective or you can create an entire lifestyle of routine surprise.

But even once Spencer and Art mixed together to produce the Post-it note, the idea wasn't complete. The first commercial launch of the product failed. The secret to their eventual success (and the reason the Post-its are still alive and well today) is iteration. 3M, the company behind Post-its, tried different ways to market the product until it hit on the catchy name "Post-it" and started handing out samples. Sometimes creativity is a sudden insight, but more often than not it is a process fueled by lots of tiny tweaks.

Iterate

Three teenage boys crouch on the floor, sawing a plank of wood that's taller than all of them combined. They've been at it for hours. Their mood has shifted steadily from enthusiasm to frustration. Their faces drip with sweat. Their knees are caked in splinters and sawdust. They've stopped making jokes and swapping stories. But when the end appears in sight, their saws move faster, and their enthusiasm returns. "Done!" one of them yells and raises his goggles in triumph. The boys celebrate with something that looks like a victory dance. They lift the wooden beam, drag it over to the rest of the structure they're building, and then they freeze. "No way," one of them mutters, "It doesn't fit."

Their instructor, an architect, stands off to the side with crossed arms and a subtle smirk. He knows the combination of disappointment, anger, and despair the boys are about to experience will be no picnic, but he also recognizes that this just might be one of the best learning experiences of their lives. They aren't really here to learn about architecture, woodworking, or model building. They are taking a course at NuVu Studio, a school that trains students to think creatively. The specific lesson they've just learned is the importance of iterating.

The boys did what most of us have been taught to do: plan, execute, hope for the best. And just as it happens in the real world, they found that their plan didn't fit reality. Instead of setting themselves up for lots of tiny surprises by testing and tweaking their ideas often, the boys grabbed their saws and got one very big unpleasant surprise at the end.

Iterating isn't just valuable in architecture. Saba Ghole, Nu-Vu's cofounder and chief creative officer, explained to us, "It's about being able to explore quickly and make your mistakes early. That's why small companies can be so competitive. They ask lots of questions, rapidly test their ideas, and make changes without wasting time or resources."

Engineering the unexpected is exciting but also intimidating. How will people react? Will the idea work? There's no way to know without trying it out. You can put your idea out into the world, make it better, see how it works, make it better again, and so on, with the understanding that most creations will need to be iterated indefinitely. A case in point: There is no such thing as a final version of Google.

REMEMBER THE SEESAW

A final word of advice about getting creative. Remember the Seesaw. Too much predictability makes us bored. Predictable ideas slip past our attention without us ever noticing. But too much surprise can make us uncomfortable, which loses our attention too. As many frustrated artists, thinkers, and inventors know: Some ideas are *too* different.

Think back to the Shift Phase of the Surprise Sequence. It's tough to let our schemata change. When something is too different from our expectations, we often ignore it. That is why Hollywood movies do well when they follow a familiar formula but have small surprises and twist endings. As Thomas Wedell-Wedellsborg told us, "Add too much surprise, and your blockbuster mutates into an art film."

On the bright side, with enough exposure, we often come around. Cars, airplanes, email, and even rolling suitcases all seemed ludicrous at one point. In 1946, film studio executive Darryl Zanuck said, "Television won't be able to hold on to any market it captures after the first six months. People will soon get tired of staring at a plywood box every night."[7] The bad news is that it can take a while for our schemata to shift. Apple products are celebrated today (with a stock value that's more than double the size of Microsoft's as of this writing), but it took Apple over a decade to pull ahead of Microsoft. For a long time, Apple was far too unconventional for the public.

So go ahead and get to curious, live in the fog, practice idea mixology, and iterate. But be gentle on your audience's schemata. Let your ideas run wild without saying no. Then remember the Seesaw and iterate to find the right balance of surprise and familiarity. Observe people's reactions to your idea. Do they shift uncomfortably or do their eyes light up? Do they change the conversation or pummel you with eager questions? Do you have to explain your idea from scratch or can you compare it to something that already exists (*It's like _____, but different.*)? If you're finding that your idea is too surprising, you have a few options: Iterate some more, find a different audience (with a different set of schemata), or be patient and wait for the world to catch up to you. Once you have your surprise ready for deployment, your next challenge is to find the attention it deserves. Let's meet in the next chapter to talk about that.

··· CHEAT SHEET ···

THE BITE-SIZE VERSION

To engineer the unexpected, we need to get creative. Creative thinking means devising new ideas and shifting our perspective to see things in surprising ways.

TOOLS

- **Get to curious:** think of curious as a place you go to rather than an emotion you feel. Get more engaged with your environment by playing the Twenty Questions game.
- **Live in the fog:** when searching for answers, tell yourself that it's okay to sit in the fog and wait for a while—the fog is where our brains generate the best ideas. Collect observations without searching for answers.
- **Practice idea mixology:** spark new ideas by inviting collisions of unrelated topics.
- **Iterate:** release ideas into the world quickly and often so that you can tweak them—get lots of small surprises instead of setting yourself up for one big unpleasant surprise.

EXERCISE YOUR SURPRISE MUSCLE

Imagine you are on the block party planning committee in your town. You have to come up with party ideas the likes of which the world has never seen. Use the tools above to get creative. What ideas do you have for making your block party a blockbuster?

Chapter Seven

Wield Attention

In the midst of working on her dissertation at the University of Vienna, LeeAnn got a call from a professor. He explained that he'd heard of her research on learning and hoped to get her help. He hesitated to go into detail but explained that the university launched a program to bring faculty research to the public. Professors had twenty minutes to share their findings, and the community was invited to attend for free. The trouble, he said, was attendance. In an auditorium of about a thousand seats, there were typically no more than fifteen audience members—a few overachieving grad students, the spouse or mother of the professor, and a handful of senior citizens looking for a place to hide from the cold.

As soon as LeeAnn attended a session, she understood the real problem. It wasn't low attendance. Attendance was low because the professors were excruciatingly boring. They stood behind the podium reading a jumble of information from presentation slides. The audience made a valiant effort to pay attention but inevitably, even the brightest of eyes glazed over. "Do you think you can help us improve the presentations?" the professor asked. "I can try," said LeeAnn.

She conducted her investigation by sitting in on lectures and surveying the meager audience to see which professors were best at getting and keeping attention. She asked attendees to rate the lecturers on a scale of 0 to 100. Most professors scored around 70 points. But some were different. Not only did they score in the 90s, their audiences actually retained the information and planned to share it with others. LeeAnn watched these attention-wielding superstars again and again until she spotted their patterns. She met with the faculty to share her findings. Most of them were skeptical. Just one professor, an anthropologist, agreed to give LeeAnn's methods a try.

The difference was immediate. By applying LeeAnn's surprise-rich techniques, the anthropologist's score leaped more than 20 points. Little by little the other faculty followed—over 150 professors from six departments. Their lectures transformed from forgettable to fascinating. Within a year, they were presenting to auditoriums without an empty seat in the house.

What follows are some of the most effective tools for wielding attention that LeeAnn picked up back in Vienna and has refined together with Tania over the years. These techniques have transformed everything from dust to gallbladders into compelling subjects. These are our favorite tools for standing apart from the crowd and keeping others engaged. They've been used by teachers, salespeople, novelists, musicians, filmmakers, designers, and parents. Even if you don't think of yourself as someone who needs to wield attention, it's likely that this skill will come in handy—especially in today's noisy world.

Engineering the unexpected begins with a bold idea. (And by "idea" we don't just mean a thought but also an innovation, service, product, or information.) But an idea isn't enough on its own. As we often find with our clients, the most important and creative ideas often stay hidden because they fail to find attention. It is these very ideas that have the power to transform people and relationships. Once an idea reaches an audience, there's no telling how far it will go and how much good it will do. This chapter stems from our passion for helping good ideas spread.

We will begin by exploring the growing significance of attention in our world, dig into the science of attention and its intimate relationship with surprise, and share attention-wielding tools that will allow you to be even more skilled in engineering the unexpected.

THE ATTENTION ECONOMY

It's six o'clock, you're hungry, your pants are too tight, and you're stuck in traffic. The last thing you want to do is pay attention to a traffic cop telling you when to go, when to stop, and where to turn. Unless of course that traffic cop is a woman by the name of Mentoria Hutchinson (aka Hutch). To get the drivers' attention, Hutch—a sixty-three-year old New Yorker—turns the Upper East Side into her personal stage and literally dances in the streets. She slides, she spins, she points her white-gloved hands disco style, and the crowd goes wild. Drivers grin, wave, and honk their horns in delight. In an interview with the *New York*

Times, Hutch said: "When you get the people's attention, you can basically get them to do anything."[1]

Hutch is right. The ability to get and keep attention is a source of power—especially today. For Hutch, all the attention has led to fan mail, YouTube videos, happy drivers, and most important, a safer job (when people pay attention to traffic enforcers, they don't drive into them). But there's a lot more you can do when you've captured attention, from reaching new customers to motivating your friends. Not long ago, only advertising agencies and news reporters obsessed over attention, but today, attention wielding is becoming a fundamental life skill for all of us.

Most societies have long believed in the power of money. But it wasn't until the 1970s that political scientists started speculating that it's not money but *attention* that is our most precious commodity, and it is quickly becoming an endangered resource. In our busy, data-saturated world, the demand for attention is so high and supply is so low that economists (like Thomas Davenport and John Beck) have taken to calling the driving force of our society the attention economy.[2]

Public speakers, salespeople, educators, and even parents used to have the time to convince their listeners that they were worthy of their attention. But these days, no matter how meaningful your message, if it doesn't stand out from the noise, it gets lost on the cutting room floor. Attention wielding isn't just a challenge for websites (where people can enter and exit guilt free). Thanks to our easy-to-conceal smartphones, teachers have to compete with the entire content of the Internet. TV programs have to compete with other TV programs (the average U.S. family has over 180 channels).[3] YouTube videos have to compete with other YouTube videos. Blogs have to outshine other blogs. And thanks to dating sites, even singles can't catch a break (there are over 40 million of them trying to get noticed online).[4]

In the past, our solution for breaking through noise was to be the loudest, flashiest, and most repetitive. Companies could pour money into billboards, commercials, and magazine ads then sit back as money rolled in. Teachers had the advantage of "owning" all the information, so students had no choice but to listen to them. Managers could bark orders at employees and expect them to obey. But today we're all competing for one another's attention second after scarce second. So how is it that even in the midst of this cutthroat competition some people and organizations still manage to get noticed? To answer this question, let's first investigate the science behind attention.

YOUR BRAIN ON ATTENTION: GETTING IT AND KEEPING IT

Imagine you hear a crash in the next room. The strange sound elicits the Freeze Phase of the Surprise Sequence: It stops you in your tracks and redirects your cognitive resources to the surprise. Next comes the Find Phase: a search for information. Ivan Pavlov (of drooling dog fame) called this the orienting response or the "What is it?" reflex.[5] Psychologists today refer to it as transient attention. That is the kind of attention we mean when we talk about *getting* attention. The transient attention that surprise triggers is instantaneous, involuntary, and different from the attention we refer to when we talk about paying attention in class or during a meeting.

The average website visitor decides whether to keep paying attention (that is, stay on the page) within ten seconds.[6] That means that if nothing causes the user to freeze and get curious, she'll take her attention elsewhere. But once she decides to stick around, she switches on a different sort of thinking called sustained attention—which is what we mean when we talk about *keeping* someone's attention.

The distinction between transient and sustained attention comes in handy when discussing attention span—a topic that's been hotly debated since researchers began to suspect that television was killing society's ability to pay attention. As the number of things demanding attention in our world grows, people have been asking, "Is our attention span shrinking?" Some researchers insist that it is, pointing to the swiftness with which we change the channel or click off a website.[7] But others believe that we are adapting to the new pace of our world and making our selections more efficiently.[8] Once we do make those selections, though, we're capable of sustaining focus for a much longer period of time.

Comedian Jerry Seinfeld has famously said, "This whole idea of an attention span is, I think, a misnomer. People have an infinite attention span if you are entertaining them."[9] And it's true that in the midst of constant attention shifting and cries of "We're all getting ADHD!" there are plenty of activities that seem to grip us indefinitely. Even a kid with a supposedly short attention span can spend hours playing a video game, watching a TV show, talking to a friend, or reading a good book.

While getting attention relies on the Freeze and Find Phase of the Surprise Sequence, keeping attention relies on the Find and Shift Phases. If what we're experiencing doesn't consistently intrigue us and offer us new perspectives, we go off in search of more interesting pastures. Throughout the rest of this chapter, we'll examine tools for getting and keeping attention so that your surprising ideas get noticed. Our goal must never be to trick people into paying attention but to present content in a way that sparks genuine curiosity and excitement. We all want to be interested. Our hope is that you will help make our world a more interesting place. You'll find many other suggestions from attention-wielding experts elsewhere, but we'll focus on the surprise-based tools that were most effective in LeeAnn's experiments at the University of Vienna and in our work beyond.

GETTING ATTENTION

As Laozi has said, a journey of a thousand miles begins with a single step. In the same way, the journey to sustained attention begins with those few seconds in which you capture transient attention. The two most effective tools we know for getting attention are interrupting patterns and creating knowledge gaps.

Interrupt Patterns

Dog dog dog dog dog dog dog cat dog dog dog dog dog dog dog.

Even if you are a dog lover, we bet the cat in the previous sentence got your attention. There's nothing particularly special about this cat other than the fact that he created a pattern interrupt. Your brain was expecting more dogs, so it was surprised to encounter a cat. This slight surprise was enough to momentarily snare your attention.

On a physiological level, the less surprising something is, the less we feel it. Imagine sitting in the movies and holding hands with someone special. At first the sensation is new and exciting, but after just a few minutes your brain becomes habituated, and you literally cannot feel the hand you're holding. To regain the sensation, you have to interrupt the pattern and change your hand position. Habituation makes sense from an evolutionary standpoint. Our ancestors survived because they prioritized new, unexpected information over familiar information. Familiarity is safe. Novelty is risky—full of both danger and opportunity.

Pattern interrupts get our attention in all walks of life, from public awareness campaigns to music. To understand why some music has an attention-gripping and chill-producing effect on listeners, researchers had participants listen to music while monitoring their heart rate and sweat levels.[10] The moments that produced a sudden physiological shift in listeners and a subjective feeling of chills had two things in common: an increase in volume from soft to loud and a sudden shift from a solo instrument (such as a violin) to the orchestra (for example, strings and woodwinds). The researchers wrote, "The music went through a harmonic progression that briefly deviated from a pattern that could have been expected based on the previous section."

To harness the power of pattern interrupts, create a pattern then give it a twist. Instructors can spend ten minutes on an exercise then have students swap seats. Designers can use a consistent color then add a splash of something unexpected. Cooks can sneak unusual bursts of flavor into an otherwise ordinary dish. Writers can craft several long sentences. Then a short one.

You can also take advantage of preexisting patterns and devise ways to interrupt them. Like Hutch, the dancing traffic enforcer. We expect a lot of behaviors from someone directing traffic but the shimmy isn't one of them. The pattern you interrupt can be small, like changing the way you answer the phone, or it can be elaborate, like Volkswagen's Fun Theory challenge. Participants in this playful contest had to capture people's attention by turning something boring into something fun. One team achieved this goal by interrupting the staircase pattern. Members of the team wanted to bring attention to the stairs and away from the escalator. Their idea: turn the stairs into piano keys that play music. The experiment worked, with 66 percent more people choosing to take the stairs than normal.[11]

Marketing departments take advantage of pattern interrupts by stamping "NEW" on anything that is even remotely changed (even if it's just a matter of mixing a few extra slices of onion into an old salsa recipe). They also understand the power of packaging an old thing in a new way (like when Shreddies "rotated" its square cereal and called it Diamond Shreddies). But most of us stick to familiarity even when attempting to grab people's attention. Anyone who has begun a presentation with "Good afternoon, everyone. I'm honored to be here today" has let an opportunity pass him by. Can you think of a better way to open? As marketing whiz Seth Godin writes, "If you want the word to spread, if you expect me to take action I've never taken before, it seems to me that you need to do something that hasn't been done before. It might not feel safe, but if you do the safe thing, I guarantee you won't surprise anyone."[12]

Create Knowledge Gaps

A gaggle of third graders huddles around a small table. They stare into a bowl of water. Vicki Cobb hands one boy a pepper shaker and tells him to shake it into the water. He does. All the kids watch, mesmerized. Vicki instructs another kid to stick his finger in the water. He does, and nothing happens. Now for the finishing move. She gives him a bit of dish soap to rub on his finger. This time, when he places it back in the water, the pepper flakes disperse like startled fish, leaving only unseasoned water in the center of the bowl. The response is immediate: "Wow!" "Oh my goodness." "Oh my gosh!"

According to Vicki (scientist, educator, and author of almost one hundred science books for kids) this reaction is typical. But what's more fascinating than the pepper surprise or even the kids' intense focus is the thing that happens next. They look up at Vicki and beg for an explanation. She fires questions right back: "Why do you think it happened? How can we figure it out?" With a mixture of spunk and a no-nonsense attitude, Vicki tells us, "When kids ask you a question, you don't tell them the answer. You have to, *have to* respond with a question. As long as they don't know the answer, they'll keep trying to figure it out." That is the essence of the attention-getting tool that we call creating knowledge gaps. Once a surprise stops us in our tracks (*That pepper didn't act like normal pepper!*), our brains try to figure out an explanation. Instinctively, we seek to close the gap between what we understand and what we don't yet know.

One of the easiest ways to create a knowledge gap is by asking questions. If your question is relevant to the listener's interests and tough to answer, you'll be rewarded with attention. This tool works in classrooms (*Why do you think things fall?*), conferences (*What's are the three core differences between businesses that succeed and ones that fail?*), conversations (*What's your favorite memory?*), and even books about surprise (*What does someone have to do to get your attention?*).

KEEPING ATTENTION

Getting attention is tough. Keeping it is tougher. To keep your listeners engaged, you have to periodically stop them in their tracks, reactivate their curiosity, challenge their schemata, and make sticking around worth the time and effort. Luckily, surprise is the secret weapon in keeping attention too. Two tools that are particularly good at keeping attention are producing predictable unpredictability and unfolding mystery.

Produce Predictable Unpredictability

The following is a list of items you'll find in a box in Ashley Albert's closet:

- Three chicken suits (two traditional; one inflatable)
- One sumo wrestler costume
- Two hundred and sixteen plastic neon-colored eggs

- Two pairs of giant sunglasses
- Two turbo bubble guns
- One confetti cannon
- Three arrow headbands

There are several boxes in Ashley's closet, each containing a different medley of similar supplies. If Alice in Wonderland and Willy Wonka had a daughter, and that daughter had a walk-in closet, it would look exactly like this. Ashley is the creator and lead singer of The Jimmies, a highly acclaimed kid indie band. The whimsical contents of these boxes help glue kids and parents to their seats at venues ranging from *Austin City Limits* to Lollapalooza.

"My mission is predictable unpredictability," Ashley tells us as we rummage through her boxes. "People should know that something's coming and have no way to guess what that something will be. If they know what's coming, then it's not special, and if it's not special then I haven't done my job." Hence the bubble guns, groundhog puppets, princess dresses (you get the picture). When describing her audience, Ashley says: "They stare up at us with this intense look of anticipation. Then when we reveal that special something, they go nuts. It's the epitome of joy. And it's pretty adorable."

This approach isn't just for the young and easily amused. Ashley's latest venture, Royal Palms Shuffleboard, New York City's first shuffleboard nightclub, is also designed with surprise in mind. From constantly changing food trucks to drag queen bingo, Royal Palms gets adults in the door and keeps their attention through the sticky power of surprise after *anticipated* surprise.

When people attend Ashley's concerts or enter her club, they know something amazing will happen. They just don't know what. When you tune in to watch your favorite TV show, you expect to be delighted by a series of surprises, whether they are creative jokes or creative murders. When you log into Facebook you are anticipating an unexpected treat in your newsfeed. And our most engaging conversations are filled with delightful discoveries, anecdotes, and insights that we had no way of predicting. Predictable unpredictability is addicting. We can't help but continue to pay attention when we are expecting something unexpected.

Along with Ashley, another prop-user we've met is educator Bobby Brooks. He travels with a portable closet and changing tent. The closet is packed with costumes such as a referee, judge, and giant yellow M&M. Bobby changes in and out of costumes as he lectures to college students about marketing. Each costume corresponds thematically to the class topic. LifeLabs New York clients—for example, professors at Columbia University Business School—create an expectation of unpredictability in a less amusing but nevertheless effective way. They call on students at random to respond to questions. As unpleasant as this tactic may seem, LeeAnn's research shows that it leads engagement and learning to skyrocket. Even students (albeit sometimes begrudgingly) admit that it works.

Last but not least, to produce predictable unpredictability, we can simply permit vulnerability. TED content director Kelly

Stoetzel and associate content producer Nick Weinberg told us that it isn't expertise but vulnerability and authenticity that distinguish engaging speakers from forgettable ones. At TED rehearsals, speakers pour far more time into exercising their ability to stay vulnerable than they spend on memorizing lines and fine-tuning posture. "It's extremely important that we let speakers show their true selves on stage," said Nick. "If they're totally geeky, let them be totally geeky. If they're loud and bouncy—let them be. This one speaker, the astronomer Clifford Stoll, has crazy hair and paces on stage and his hair flops everywhere, and it's brilliant because you can feel his passion and his energy."

We know what to expect from guarded, scripted individuals—we expect them to play it safe and stick to the conventional patterns of our society. As soon as we get the sense that these folks are predictable, they become neurologically invisible to us. But when someone is vulnerable we sense that anything is possible, and we can't help but lean in and pay attention.

Unfold Mystery

"The rest of Harry's sentence was drowned out by a high-pitched mewling from somewhere near his ankles. He looked down and found himself gazing into a pair of lamp-like yellow eyes. It was Mrs. Norris, the skeletal gray cat." This is a passage from J. K. Rowling's *Harry Potter and the Chamber of Secrets*. We opened the book and selected this excerpt at random, but it is a perfect representation of her writing style. It is also a clue to what makes her books so compulsively readable (and what distinguishes them from the most tedious teachers at the University of Vienna). J. K. uses a method we call unfolding mystery.

Unfolding mystery is like weaving a chain of knowledge gaps, fueling and refueling the Find and Shift Phases. Notice that J. K. doesn't say there was a cat mewling at Harry's feet. Instead, she pulls us in and makes us stick around to discover the source of the unexpected sound (even if we suspected all along that it was the cat). Sentence after sentence and chapter after chapter, she plants questions in our minds that keep us turning to the next page in search of the answers. Imagine feeding your dog a hamburger one crumble at a time. When you hand over the whole treat, the burger disappears and the fun ends there. When it's broken up into pieces, your dog gets more and more excited with every meaty bite. This principle applies to stomachs and to minds.

One of the best approaches to unfolding mystery is story. As soon we hear the words *let me tell you a story*, we lean just a bit closer to the speaker. It's irresistible. Even a story that you wouldn't describe as surprising has surprise and wonder at its core. A story is a promise. When you say "Once upon a time" (or one of its modern equivalents), you are promising your listeners that *something* will happen. They have to keep listening to find out what. Award-winning director J. J. Abrams likens this process to planting mystery boxes for his audience to unwrap.[13]

Andrew Stanton (cocreator of *Toy Story* and *WALL-E*) firmly believes that audiences actually want to work to figure out what happens next and what it all means.[14] They want to do the tough mental labor of wondering. Andrew and his colleague at Pixar,

Bob Peterson, call this concept the Unifying Theory of 2 + 2. In their experience, audiences don't want to be given 4. They want to be given 2 + 2 and to figure out 4 on their own. Similarly, education researcher David Johnson says that the gradual unfolding of information in the classroom through surprise and mystery "characterizes the difference between the teacher who uncovers the subject as compared with the teacher who covers the textbook."[15]

There may come a time when you are holding an idea in your hands that you believe in with all your heart. But the world doesn't seem to notice it. Your first instinct may be to climb atop the highest structure in the room and shout. Before you clear your throat, take a small pause. Ask yourself whether your message is right for this audience. Just because we have something to say, it doesn't mean people owe us their attention. Next, consider whether you are being strategic and intentional in engineering the unexpected. Think back to the tools in your arsenal: interrupting patterns, creating knowledge gaps, producing predictable unpredictability, and unfolding mystery. When the professors at the University of Vienna (whom you met at the start of this chapter) didn't get attention, their impulse was to speak louder and add more slides to their presentation. It took patience and practice to finally wield attention in that auditorium. Once they did, their ideas reverberated throughout the community.

THE BITE-SIZE VERSION
Getting attention means stopping people in their tracks and sparking their curiosity. Keeping attention requires planting many small surprises and stretching the wonder.

TOOLS
· **Interrupt patterns:** create a pattern then give it a twist, or spot an existing pattern and do something different from what people expect.
· **Create knowledge gaps:** show people there is something they don't know yet and that they have to keep listening to get the answer.
· **Produce predictable unpredictability:** establish an expectation that a surprise will come—though no one should know when or how.
· **Unfold mystery:** use suspense to your advantage. Instead of presenting information all at once, reveal it little by little.

EXERCISE YOUR SURPRISE MUSCLE
You have to give a presentation on the concepts you just read about in this book. Your audience consists of executives who insist that they have very little time. They're all armed with smartphones and get easily distracted. How can you get and keep their attention?

Chapter Eight

Design Delight

After an intense collaboration between *Sesame Street* and IDEO's Toy Lab, it was time to place the designers' idea into the hands of the experts: the toddlers. And not just any toddlers—two- and three-year-olds who hate nothing more than potty training. When *Sesame Street* asked the Toy Lab to help kids (and parents) survive potty training, they knew it would be one of their toughest challenges yet. The problem seems simple enough—get your kid to poop in a pot—but parents, psychoanalysts, and anyone in the multi-million dollar toilet training industry will tell you that there's nothing simple about this stage in a child's life.

The Toy Lab devised a potty training app. When the first prototype was complete, parents handed smartphones to their kids and observed their behavior. Though the app was colorful, musical, and jam-packed with features to help kids learn about potty training, just one button got most of the attention. The "summon Elmo" button "dialed" Elmo's number, and his face popped up on a screen identical to a video call. Kids could see their faces on the call too, giving them the sense that they were talking directly to Elmo just as they would to Grandma. It was a huge surprise. Toddlers giggled, grinned, and eagerly listened to Elmo's potty training tips.

The designers revamped the app (which now goes by the name Elmo Calls) to consist only of voice and video calls. Elmo talks about frustrating things like using the potty, brushing your teeth, and bathing. Amazingly, kids actually listen. The new version of the app even allows parents to schedule calls so that Elmo calls you. Can you imagine getting a personal call from your favorite celebrity? This joyful surprise turns a previously unpleasant activity like using the potty (or perhaps in your case, doing your taxes) into something fun. What's more, the positive surprise inspires kids to talk to Elmo again and again. Within less than a year of the app's release, Elmo had made over 100 million calls.

The success of the app spells clear benefits to parents in the throes of potty training about the power of the unexpected. But parents and toddlers are just a pixel in the big picture. Positive surprise can have a transformative effect on all of us. In the previous chapter we talked about the importance of wielding attention to engineer the unexpected. Without attention, your message may as well be playing on mute. Elmo certainly captures attention, but he goes one step further. He creates delight. *Delight* is the word psychologists use to describe pleasant surprise.[1]

Delight allows us to reach one another on an emotional level, not just an attentional one. Emotion inspires action and creates connection. Delight feels wonderful for recipients and surprise makers alike, and that's the best reason in the world to take it seriously. But if you ever have to convince a skeptic that designing delight is well worth the effort, consider some of its other benefits.

A study of hotel reviews on TripAdvisor found that "very satisfied" guests were only 24 percent more likely than merely "satisfied" guests to stay at the hotel again and recommend it to others.[2] But guests who reported experiencing a "delightful surprise" were 58 percent more likely to repurchase and recommend than simply satisfied guests. And an entire 97 percent of individuals who felt delightful surprise expressed loyalty to the hotel. Just like toddlers who wanted more and more calls from Elmo, delighted guests wanted to stay at the hotel again and again.

Delight triggers the Share Phase of the Surprise Sequence, inspiring individuals to talk about their experiences with an average of six listeners.[3] Of course, in an age of social media, that number can rapidly turn into six thousand. Delightful surprise is the greatest driver of positive word of mouth. Delight shifts our perspective about unpleasant and neutral activities (like using the potty or going to the gym or doing homework), paving the way for healthy new behaviors. It can also improve productivity. Researchers have found that a positive mood is most conducive for creative problem solving.[4] Seeing as our world is becoming increasingly dependent on new ideas, it stands to reason that we can all use more delight in our homes and workplaces. Finally, when we design delight, we show people that they matter enough to us to put effort and energy into surprising them. (This message comes across even if our master plan gets slightly botched along the way.) Doesn't everyone deserve to be reminded every once in a while that someone cares?

When we engineer the unexpected, we turn the ordinary into the extraordinary. When we design delight, we go a step further. We turn the extraordinary into the extraordinarily meaningful and memorable. In this chapter we'll explain the science of delight and then share our favorite tools for engineering the *delightfully* unexpected. We'll also discuss how to create a sustainable surprise system for designing delight. You can apply these tools to any area of life and work. If delight can make poop more fun, the possibilities are endless.

THE EXPECTATION BAR

Imagine you've just ordered a plain toasted bagel with cream cheese. You pay for your breakfast, take the warm aluminum-wrapped parcel from the cashier, and head out the door. Once you get to work, you unwrap the foil and find . . . a plain toasted bagel with cream cheese. What do you feel? Unless the store has a habit of getting your order wrong, you feel very little. This moment in your life is so unimportant that your brain hardly processes it. When events go as planned, they meet *the expectation bar.*

Now, let's say you unwrap the foil to find a partially frozen onion bagel with butter. Egh. This event falls below your expectation bar, which means you are negatively surprised or, to put it simply, disappointed. On the other hand, if you unwrap the foil and find that the store has tucked in *two* perfectly toasted bagels with cream cheese at no extra charge (and you aren't counting calories), the event falls above your expectation bar. You are pleasantly surprised. You are delighted.

Delight and disappointment are closely linked with the neurotransmitter dopamine. By studying monkeys' neural reactions to unexpected squirts of fruit juice (because monkeys love juice), neuroscientist Wolfram Schultz found that events above the expectation bar release dopamine in the brain and events below the bar diminish dopamine.[5] Although dopamine is often associated with pleasure, scientists now suspect that this connection isn't exactly correct. There's a difference between liking and wanting. When animal and human research subjects are treated with drugs that block or deplete dopamine, they still seem to experience pleasure but not desire.[6] Dopamine is the wanting drug. So when it comes to delight, it doesn't merely produce pleasure but also triggers the desire for more. That may be why delight can transform tasks we don't like into activities we want to repeat. It also explains why companies and individuals (Elmo included) who manage to delight us keep us coming back. On the other hand, disappointment teaches us to lower our expectations and stay away.

Throughout our careers as Surprisologists, we've helped design delight into a wide range of situations from conferences to products and even into the city of Brindisi, Italy. Regardless of project scope, we've found that every effective design begins with an understanding of the expectation bar. Whether you are plotting surprises for your kids or for your customers, if you aren't empathizing with people's expectations, your attempts at delight will be about as strategic as playing darts in the dark.

It's also important to remember that not all delight is made equal. A car with windows that open and close much faster than expected might produce a burst of delight, but there are expectation bars that drivers value far more than window speed (like comfort, safety, price, and fuel economy). A friend who buys us gifts might delight us, but the much more important expectation bar in friendship is usually honesty and dependability. To strengthen the friendship, these expectation bars need far more attention.

Any attempt at designing delight must begin with tracking the most meaningful expectation bars. One of the best ways to track expectations is to pay careful attention to what people say. At Surprise Industries, LifeLabs New York, and in our personal lives, any time people mention something they find important or special we jot it down in a top-secret spreadsheet called the Surprise File. We visit it periodically to find opportunities to design delight. (You'll find your very own Surprise File at the end of this book.)

Complaints can be even more helpful because they reveal low expectations (opportunities to reach above the bar). If you notice that your spouse is perpetually frustrated by your lack of dish washing or your staff grumbles about inconvenient work hours, you've already spotted opportunities for delight. Just think of how Netflix took advantage of our chronically low expectations for video rentals (paying painful late fees and trudging outside to pick up a movie). By surpassing these deep-seated expectations through a mail-order service, Netflix delighted millions of grateful customers.

DELIGHT DESIGN TOOLS

Once we've tracked down the most meaningful expectations, we simply have to surpass the bar. There are infinite ways to design delight, but these are three of our favorite tools: under promise/over deliver, bury a cookie, and give just because.

Under Promise/Over Deliver

A luxury goods retailer with one of the world's best reputations and some of the world's finest-quality clothing, had a problem. On the very same street as the company's flagship store there were *four* other luxury goods stores also enjoying the world's best reputations and clothing quality. To a customer with money to spend and just the right mood for trying on evening gowns, the store was virtually indistinguishable from the others. And it wasn't until one unlikely client walked through its shiny glass doors that the company realized how it could stand out and build stronger relationships with clients.

Miriam entered clutching a weather-beaten purse with a torn strap. She placed it on the counter without letting go and spoke without looking up to meet the salesperson's eyes. "Look, I bought this bag seven years ago, and I know it's way too expensive for me. I wasn't even going to ask if you could fix it, but I love it. It's the nicest thing I've ever owned." Cora—the sales associate behind the counter—was deeply moved by Miriam's honesty and her attachment to the bag. She couldn't afford it either (a $2,800 purchase), and she understood the confidence and pride Miriam felt when she slung it over her shoulder before heading out to face the world. She told Miriam that the repair would be $50—a price that made Miriam wince but only a little, and she promised to have the bag ready for pickup next week.

When Miriam returned, she was giddy with anticipation, but what she found waiting for her on the counter wasn't her familiar beat-up bag. It was a gleaming, freshly stitched purse that looked as new as the day she bought it. Not only had Cora fixed the strap, she also had the entire bag cleaned and restitched. Miriam's first reaction was panic. "I didn't ask for all that. I can't afford it," she stammered. Then when Cora handed her the invoice—a total of $25—Miriam burst into tears. It wasn't just that she was relieved to save some money or excited to get a shiny, new-looking bag. To Miriam, the bag represented being seen, valued, and respected. She walked out of the store thoroughly delighted.

A few days later, she wrote a letter that made its way up to the president of the company. From that point on, something shifted in the culture of the store. Instead of focusing on satisfying customers, the sales and operations teams became obsessed with spotting opportunities to engineer delight. Not just because it was good for business but, as one team member explained, "It was good for the soul." Employees began thinking of themselves as agents of delight rather than employees. And they stopped looking at customers as customers and started looking at them as people. The only problem was that it got expensive. Before long, the store burned through its "delight budget," and the choice became return to business as usual or find a way to delight for free.

To solve this riddle, the team looked back on their experience with Miriam. The more they thought about it, the more clearly they saw that it wasn't the clean bag that moved Miriam to tears but the fact that she wasn't expecting it to be cleaned. She was only expecting a fixed strap (along with cold, impersonal customer service). By surpassing her expectations, Cora showed that Miriam was important to her. Without realizing it, the team stumbled on what business management consultant Tom Peters has called the formula for success: under promise/ over deliver.

Most of us do the opposite. We compulsively over promise and under deliver. "Come try the world's best pizza" we say to describe mediocre slices. "I'll get this to you by Monday" we say, then procrastinate until Wednesday. "I'll be five minutes late," we swear even though we're secretly sure we won't get there for another half hour. While over promising makes us look good at first, it ultimately results in disappointment. Under promising harnesses the power of misexpected surprise. It makes us look okay at first, but then it results in delight, which benefits everyone involved.

The goal isn't to set the expectation bar low (*We've got the world's worst pizza, everybody!*) but just an inch or two lower than what you plan to deliver. Some companies do this with shipping estimates, promising a product in two days but sending it overnight. Spouses can under promise/over deliver with dinner plans—setting expectations for mushy leftovers but cooking a delicious hot meal instead. For the luxury-goods store, the under promise/over deliver philosophy made delight consistently accessible and best of all, absolutely free—all they had to do was nudge down the expectation bar then leap above it.

Bury a Cookie

There are companies that are pretty good, companies that are fantastic, and then there are the companies that we fall in love with. We suspect that whenever love is in the air, delight is the cupid. Our friend Benjamin has been carrying on a love affair with the Kimpton Hotel in Boston for over ten years. He drives there even if it's hours out of his way, and he's talked about it with everyone he's ever met. The catalyst for Benjamin's obsession happened at the tail end of his first stay. He checked out and asked the valet to bring his car. He was driving for nearly ten minutes when he noticed something tucked into his dashboard. What he found was a box with a still-warm chocolate chip cookie and a handwritten note wishing him a safe trip home. Whether or not actual cookies are involved, we like to call this delight design practice burying a cookie. While under promise/over deliver relies on misexpected surprise, the buried cookie is an entirely unexpected (and equally delightful) surprise.

Websites often bury cookies in the form of Easter eggs. Type the word "askew" or "tilt" into the Google search bar or "do the Harlem shake" into the YouTube search bar and see what happens. Even if you've never come across these hidden delights, you're probably familiar with Google's logo, redesigned at random intervals with playful images and games.

Buried cookies can also inspire action. One office manager told us that the only surefire way to get her colleagues to answer her email and do what she asks is to bury a cookie in the form of a joke, fun fact, photo, or GIF. The surprises she slips into her communication aren't just motivating, they also make her job more fun and deepen her relationship with her colleagues.

Research supports the idea that delight spurs action. As part of an experiment, psychologist Randy Garner sent faculty members at his university surveys about their opinions on campus climate.[7] Only he wasn't the slightest bit interested in what they thought. What he wanted to find out was whether a small, personal touch (a tiny buried cookie) would motivate the faculty to respond faster. He sent one group of teachers a survey with a typed cover letter. He sent another group the same survey but stuck on a Post-it with a handwritten request and a thank you. Of the faculty who didn't get a Post-it, only 36 percent returned the survey. The Post-it group had an admirable 76 percent response rate.

One of the best opportunities to bury a cookie is in spots where expectations and moods are low. Many websites do this well by making their 404 (error) page funny. Instead of being frustrated, users are actually delighted. Using the same philosophy, a restaurant called Sweetgreen tucked gift certificates into the windshields of drivers who had gotten parking tickets. And in a more elaborate stunt, the airline Spanair timed its delight perfectly on late Christmas Eve flights. Recognizing that passengers felt tired and probably a little sad traveling on a holiday, they sent personalized gifts down the conveyor belt along with the luggage.

Think of all the places you can bury cookies. In your email, boring forms, waiting rooms, your home? Just a single Post-it note and a brief caring message can do wonders. In case you are getting inspired to think bigger, we'll add a small note of caution. Remember that surprise intensifies emotion, and big surprises may be too overwhelming. Individuals from some cultures feel uncomfortable or guilty when receiving gifts—especially from a business.[8] And even in cultures where gifts are more readily appreciated, there's a reason we recommend buried cookies instead of buried Rolex watches. Smaller is usually better when it comes to delight. Aside from being too intense, a big surprise can also trigger the reciprocity norm, leading people to feel they have to find a way to pay you back instead of just enjoying the surprise. And it doesn't hurt that small delights such as sweets and sweet gestures are also less expensive and easier to pull off.

Give Just Because

If you've ever given someone a gift on a day that isn't a holiday, that person probably stared at you with the Duh Face and asked, "Why?" You triggered the Freeze and the Find Phases of the Surprise Sequence. But if you gave an explanation (*Because*

I wanted to thank you for all your hard work.), you missed out on the full potential of the delightful surprise. If you're hoping to make your gift or gesture as delightful as possible, the best justification to give anyone for your actions is "just because."

Remember that as soon as we close the Find Phase of the Surprise Sequence with an answer, we stop seeking an explanation. Researchers at the University of Virginia and Harvard University were curious how ending the search or prolonging it affects delight.[9] They were particularly fascinated by the role of randomness in random acts of kindness. To explore this question, they handed out two types of cards to students at the library. Each card contained a gold dollar, the message: "This is for you! Have a nice day!" and some brief information about the "Smile Society." But the two cards were subtly different. The "explained" cards pointed out the society and its mission with the words "Who are we?" and "Why do we do this?" The "just-because" cards kept this information vague.

Next, a different researcher approached the students and asked them to fill out an "unrelated" questionnaire about their mood. The results? Students who received the mysterious just-because cards were in a significantly better mood than students who felt they understood why they got the card. The delighted and mystified participants also thought about the card much longer than the students in the explained condition, and they remembered the text more accurately.

As the prediction paradox (mentioned in Chapter 5) predicts, most students believed that understanding the reason behind the gift would make them happier. The opposite was true. When something good happens to us we *want* to know why, but finding out diminishes our delight. Just like letters from secret admirers and small acts of kindness from strangers, the more random and inexplicable the act, the longer we'll feel good about it and the more delightful it will be.

Our perspective may seem to fly in the face of conventional thinking. Especially in the workplace, rewards typically exist to train employees to do the right thing. We give bonuses for productivity and gift cards for team spirit as though we were training dogs to do tricks. Ironically, by using extrinsic rewards to motivate good behavior, we squeeze our intrinsic motivation, making activities less enjoyable for their own sake. Sure, a Starbucks gift card can make us smile, but doing good work simply for the sake of doing good work is far more rewarding. Giving just-because surprises respects people's intrinsic drives and reminds them that they matter to us regardless of their sales numbers. The same goes for personal relationships. Birthday gifts, wedding gifts, and apology gifts are easy for our brains to explain, so they quickly lose their magic. Give someone a compliment, back rub, or present just because and see what happens.

SUSTAINABLE SURPRISE

When we get into conversations about designing delight, people's reactions are pretty predictable. At first they get excited, then they get noticeably nervous, and finally they turn downright grumbly. After listening to Tania's keynote address on delight, one CEO said, "I made a big mistake a long time ago, and I've been regretting it ever since. The phone rang after five one night, and I picked it up. Ever since then, my clients are expecting me to pick up later and later. This delight stuff is dangerous."

We've seen couples, parents, and managers experience the same frustration when they try to design delight on their own. And for good reason: Every time you give people more than they expect, you raise their expectation bar, making them harder to delight and easier to disappoint. Gifts, praise, and bonuses quickly transform from luxury into necessity. The more you delight people, the higher that bar goes. For this reason, many people actively avoid delight and simply focus on meeting expectations. We hope you'll agree that this is a sad compromise.

There are at least two ways to counteract the creeping expectation bar and create sustainable surprise. First: vary how you delight people. Chocolate and roses administered over and over again lose their romance. But different desserts and different flowers every time keep the dopamine coming. A $1 daisy following a $10 rose is worth more than yet another $10 rose.

Another way to keep surprise sustainable is by creating a random reinforcement schedule. To understand this concept, it helps to think of cats and slot machines. If you've ever lived with a cat, you probably know that many cat owners are forced into a morning ritual that, once launched, appears to have no undo button. At a certain hour every day (invariably before your alarm goes off) your cat demands food. At some point in your cohabitation you try to stop the cycle and refuse to feed Fluffy when he yowls and scratches by your door, but this only makes things worse. By rewarding the pleas for kibble, then ignoring them, and then rewarding them again, you have fed Fluffy a struggle sandwich (remember Chapter 3?) and taught him to expect that his efforts will eventually be rewarded.

The same psychological process fuels the lure of slot machines. Sometimes you get a reward, but most times you don't. It is the very randomness of this reinforcement schedule that keeps you yanking the handle. Every time you don't win, you're disappointed and frustrated, but the possibility of winning keeps you glued to your seat. Then if you ever do win—even if it's only a handful of coins—you shriek with delight while your brain is doused in dopamine. If left unchecked, this cycle can lead to addiction. But in the right hands and for the right reasons, random reinforcement creates sustainable delight.

The online grocery store FreshDirect uses random reinforcement by sneaking an extra bottle of olive oil or a bundle of free samples into its customers' deliveries. It gives away these freebies so rarely and so randomly that customers never learn to take them for granted. Want to reward your kids for doing the dishes? Random reinforcement works best here as well. Constant delight quickly turns into a salary but unexpected rewards sustain the power of surprise.

If you're worried that strategy will take the delight out of delighting, just take a look at a two-year-old talking to Elmo. More important, think about the value of delight. Sure it can trigger positive word of mouth and build loyalty, but that's just icing on the cake. The real reason to design delight is simply to delight people. In our stressful, busy, lonely, numbing world, engineering the unexpected to make someone's day is one of the most meaningful things we can do.

THE BITE-SIZE VERSION

When we trigger delight we create loyalty, catalyze word of mouth, increase productivity, and turn ordinary into extraordinary. Delight also makes people feel good, which is reason enough to take it seriously. To design delight, spot where the most meaningful expectation bars lie and surpass them.

TOOLS

- **Under promise/over deliver:** set expectations just an inch or two lower than you plan to deliver, then give people more than they expect.
- **Bury a cookie:** leave a small surprise where people aren't expecting it (in your email, your meals, and even your outfits).
- **Give just because:** intensify delight by giving with no explanation.

EXERCISE YOUR SURPRISE MUSCLE

Your friend recently opened a restaurant. She is looking for ideas to delight her customers. Use the tools above. What surprising ideas do you propose, you surprise maker you?

Make Experiences

How many people actually like eating turkey? Judging by average sales in the United States, the outlook seems bleak for the turkey meat industry. Though demand for turkey is growing, chicken remains the far more famous fowl. Then comes November. You enter your previously serene, well-stocked supermarket and you see customers scurrying about and dashing to the registers like running backs with twenty-pound footballs tucked under their arms. What triggers American taste buds to take this strange and sudden turn? The answer, of course, is that turkey is an integral part of the Thanksgiving experience. Americans don't really care to eat the turkey; they just want to *experience* it. What makes turkey delicious on Thanksgiving isn't its flavor but the role it plays in a day that's filled with small surprises.

Now consider a phenomenon that plays out year-round and worldwide. The cost of coffee beans to brew in your home is a few cents per cup. Stop by a corner store for a ready-to-drink cup and it will cost you around $1. Get a cup of the same coffee at a trendy café, and the cost doubles (or quintuples, depending on where you go). Why? When you're purchasing coffee beans you are paying for a commodity. When you get a cup of coffee at a store, you are getting a service. And when you sip your coffee at a café while looking out at the bustling street and chatting with your friend, you are paying for an experience.

The difference between commodity, service, and experience lies in the amount of surprise you feel when interacting with it. Whether it is an object or an activity, if you get exactly what you expect again and again, you end up with a commodity. Going to a fast-food restaurant is technically an experience, but it begins to feels like a commodity if we have the same experience every time. On the other hand, while a painting is only an object, it functions as an experience if it continues to surprise you by inspiring new thoughts and emotions each time you look at it.

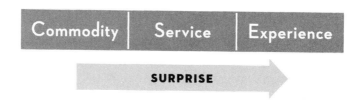

The distance between commodities, services, and experiences is more than a matter of how much you can charge for it (though that's not a bad reason to think about making experiences). More important, because experiences are rich with surprise, they hold the key to building stronger relationships and more vibrant memories. Experience-making is one of the most important tools in a surprise engineer's toolkit. In this chapter we'll use surprise as a lens to further explore what an experience is and why experiences are becoming so important. Then we'll share our very own recipe for harnessing the power of the unexpected to make experiences.

WHAT ARE EXPERIENCES AND WHY DO THEY MATTER?

In everyday language, we use the noun *experience* to mean "something that happened to us." In this sense, everything we interact with or observe is an experience. That is not how we'll be using the word *experience* in this chapter. Increasingly, economists, designers, entertainers, educators, and even scientists are making a distinction between objects and events that are experiential from those that are not.

Here is how we see the line between the experiential and nonexperiential: While commodities (such as grapes), goods (such as wine), and services (such as someone pouring you wine) are all predictable, experiences are inherently surprising. They are personal, subjective events bursting with the unknown and the unexpected. Even traditional experiences like Thanksgiving maintain their richness thanks to the power of surprise. Think of any major holiday—Christmas, Halloween, Hanukkah, your birthday; they all contain elements of cozy predictability but just as important, the promise of surprise. The most popular traditions are gift-wrapped in questions like: *What am I going to get? Who am I going to see?* And best of all, *What am I going to eat?* Experiences are exciting and immersive—triggering and retriggering our Surprise Sequence so that we are constantly paying attention, wondering, reworking our beliefs, and sharing what we've seen, thought, and felt.

B. Joseph Pine and James H. Gilmore, authors of *The Experience Economy*, put it this way: "Commodities are [replaceable], goods tangible, services intangible, and experiences memorable."[1] Because experiences linger and make us flex our schemata, they come to define our relationships and even our identities. The power of experience is important in the consumer context because experiences affect how we feel about products, services, and companies. And experiences deeply influence our personal lives.

The more experiences we have with others, the closer our relationships become. Filling our lives with experiences rather than things can even increase our happiness. As psychologists Elizabeth Dunn, Daniel Gilbert, and Timothy Wilson write, "After devoting days to selecting the perfect hardwood floor to install in a new condo, homebuyers find their once beloved Brazilian cherry floors quickly become nothing more than the unnoticed ground beneath their feet. In contrast, their memory of seeing a baby cheetah at dawn on an African safari continues to provide delight."[2]

While the hardwood floors are just that, hardwood floors, the African safari consists of myriad sensations, emotions, and surprises. So the saying "Money can't buy happiness" isn't exactly true. You actually can buy happiness if you spend your money on experiences. As Elizabeth put it in a *New York Times* interview, given the same amount of money, "it's better to go on a vacation than buy a new couch."[3]

The lure of experiences is on the rise. In a 2006 report, Trendwatching wrote that consumers increasingly "want to be surprised, moving from one ephemeral experience to another, constantly trading in the fading for the blossoming."[4] Since that report, the trend has continued, leading to increased spending in travel and education, even in tough economic times.[5]

Why the growing interest in experiences? In his book *A Whole New Mind*, psychologist Daniel Pink argues that because so many of us have met our basic needs, we have begun to search for meaning and transcendence—both of which are accessible through experiences.[6] The freeze-inducing and curiosity-sparking qualities of surprise allow experiences to pull us into the moment. The Shift Phase leads us to grow. The Share Phase allows us to feel more in tune with others. A case in point, research on romantic relationships reveals that the happiest couples have a habit of reminiscing about their shared past experiences and laughing about them together.[7]

Of course all this time we've been talking about experiences as though they were exclusively positive. Anyone who's ever been wedged in a tiny airplane seat between two onion-scented individuals while bumping and dipping through turbulence knows that not all experiences (just as not all surprises) are made equal. As the authors of *The Experience Economy* point out, "The easiest way to turn a service into an experience is to provide poor service."[8] The less we consider the importance of experience, the more likely we are to inadvertently create unpleasant ones. So how can we make experiences intentionally and skillfully?

EXPERIENCE-MAKING TOOLS

After crafting over 2,500 surprise experiences at Surprise Industries and dozens of workshops at LifeLabs New York, we think we've figured out a thing or two about experience making. In the rest of this chapter, we'll show you our experience recipe, based on the science of surprise: create a red thread, activate the senses, cocreate, and map the journey.

Create a Red Thread

A few years ago, we were guests at a Japanese tea ceremony. It took place in a small room with a low ceiling and a tatami floor that smelled like freshly cut straw. We removed our shoes and sat on our heels in wonder-filled silence. After a few moments, the shoji screen slid open with a soft *shhh* and our host bowed. She slipped into the room and positioned herself before us with an array of kettles, bowls, powders, and wooden instruments. She closed the door, and the ceremony began.

To this day we can still reexperience the earthy scents, the swishing sound of our host's blue-green kimono sleeves, and the warmth and smoothness of the cups pressed into our palms. When we recall just one component of the experience, the entire experience returns.

Contrast this immersion in the majesty of tea with another

event we attended a few weeks later. This time, we stumbled into a rooftop party in Brooklyn. There was fire eating, barbequing, and painting (and was that group humming?). It was certainly immersive, but we walked away disoriented and a little woozy. As far as we could tell, there was nothing that tied all the components of the event together. The hosts failed to use an experience-making tool we call creating a red thread.

A red thread is an idea that runs across the experience to pull it all together. Anytime a participant feels lost or overwhelmed, he can grasp the string in his mind and make sense of what he's experiencing. When clients come to us for help with making their conferences, events, and workplaces more experiential, they assume that we'll begin by weaving in surprise. In actuality, we've found that the best first step is tending to the certainty side of the Surprise Seesaw. That is the role of the red thread. When it's clear how everything in the experience ties together, participants allow themselves to venture farther into the unknown and savor the surprises.

A theme, story, topic, question, or even color can work as a red thread. As adults, we tend to think of themes as cheesy— probably because we've been to one too many luau- or poker-themed parties. But think about how excited people get about board game nights, TV show season-finale parties, and Super Bowl parties. Even holidays are theme parties at their core. Our fellow surprise maker Hannah Kane specializes in creating theme parties for adults. Her company, Everybody's Invited!, has made experiences around the themes of space travel, marshmallows, deer, and the Beatles' White Album. Every new theme inspires people to interact differently and experience the event more fully.

You can make your red thread explicit, but unspoken red threads can also do wonders to make an experience. The café chain Le Pain Quotidien uses the founder's childhood as its through line. Everything, from the rough wooden tables to the large cups (designed to be held with both hands), is inspired by Alain Coumont's memories of growing up in Belgium. Most customers don't know this story, yet they sense that something ties the experience together.

A red thread can even make work more experiential. We help our clients uncover their values and mission then amplify them by creating visible artifacts. This exercise works with individuals, teams, and entire companies. You can create a red thread through your own work by selecting a theme, object, or value that you want to focus on for one week. A clear (and inspiring) red thread can take us to surprising new places and make our experiences more meaningful and memorable.

Activate the Senses

Talk to Cirque du Soleil fans and they'll tell you that Cirque isn't just a circus; it's an experience. Every act is jam-packed with surprises, from superhuman balancing feats to seat-gripping trapeze stunts. But what most audience members don't realize is that the surprises at Cirque aren't just the spectacular sights. Scents, tastes, sounds, and physical sensations are all part of the experience. Cirque du Soleil company manager Jeff Lund told us that every detail of every show is designed to activate the senses, from the buttery smell of popcorn permeating the tents to the complex textures of the sets.

After creating a red thread, the next experience-making tool to brandish is activating the senses. You may remember that our senses pull in the most information from our environments when we feel surprise and anticipation. The more senses an experience triggers, the more fully we become immersed in the moment. Just think of the difference between working out and working out while listening to the *Rocky* theme song. Or the difference between seeing fresh bread and seeing it while also inhaling its aroma and hearing that crackle it makes when you break a piece off. Even writers and filmmakers activate the senses through description and visualization.

When we ask our workshop participants to spot something that surprises their senses, they report experiencing the environment with more intensity. You can try it for yourself by stirring up your senses one at a time and seeing what you discover. If you take a big whiff of the air, what scents do you notice that you weren't aware of before? If you scan the room now, how many different colors can you spot? When you turn your attention to your skin, how warm, cold, or humid does the air feel? Voluntarily activating our senses pulls us into the moment and reboots our attentiveness.

Of course, it's also important to keep in mind that activated senses aren't necessarily happy senses. Mixing the taste of cupcakes with the smell of cologne might be an experience, but not a pleasant one (which explains why Smell-O-Vision never got off the ground). To make effective experiences, experiment with sensory combinations that are unexpected but also enjoyable.

Like most creative endeavors, bringing surprising new experiences into the world requires a little risk taking and a lot of trial and error.

Cocreate

Every year since 1986, strangers spend one week living together outside in the brutal heat and cold of the Nevada desert. They create elaborate structures and art pieces. Then they get rid of all the evidence and return to their ordinary lives. This event is called Burning Man, and it has become so popular that the festival coordinators struggle to obtain permits allowing all interested individuals to attend. In 1997, there were roughly 10,000 participants. Within three years the number jumped to 25,000. By 2013, around 68,000 individuals participated in Burning Man.[9]

Burning Man perfectly exemplifies our third experience-making tool: cocreate. At Burning Man this concept is known as "radical participation." Nobody goes to the festival to watch from the sidelines. If you go, you do. For Burning Man organizers, this philosophy means giving up control of their event and embracing surprise. Participants sense the unpredictability and can't help but feel more fully immersed.

Even if you aren't plotting an experience as epic as Burning Man, cocreating with your participants can be scary. It means making the experience only up to a point and trusting that others will fill the space that you've left for them. If you are designing an experience for your customers, this tool may be particularly hard to stomach. In business, our impulse is to have complete control. Cocreating an experience means inviting in surprise. How can you let customers in the driver's seat without setting everyone up for a ten-car pileup?

Some companies, like merchants that let you customize your purchases, use this tool by designing in a small amount of wiggle room. Others, like companies that have unscripted customer service, handle the uncertainty by hiring people they trust to represent their values no matter what turn the experience takes. Still others, like unconference producers, just let go of the reins and see what happens.

Cocreating experiences is also valuable (though occasionally bloodcurdling) in the classroom. Educators feel safest when they know exactly what to expect, but students learn best when they take an active role, navigate ambiguity, and produce surprise. Tania faced this struggle in her first year of teaching college freshmen.

It was about two weeks into the semester and Tania was finally getting the hang of things when she opened the door to her classroom and walked into darkness. Someone had turned off the lights, and it was literally pitch black. Immediately, two voices spoke up in her head. One said (quite reasonably): "Find the switch and turn on the lights." The other said: "Let them create this experience with you." For some reason, she listened to the second voice.

Somehow she made it to the front of the class and, in the darkness, she asked her students what might be easier to talk about with the lights out. After a few minutes of giggles and chair creaks, someone suggested going around the room to share personal stories of prejudice. Again, the reasonable voice said: "That can get out of hand," but the other voice said: "Let's see what happens." And they did. For one hour the students talked in the dark with more thoughtfulness, originality, and mutual respect than they had ever revealed in class before.

From that day on something shifted in the classroom culture and in Tania's approach to teaching. By letting the students cocreate the lesson, she let the surprise in, and she let the experience grow into something that inspired the students and especially herself. Since then her lesson plans have transformed from carefully plotted bullet points to looser plans with invitations built in to change course and take a new direction together. After six years of teaching, she's convinced that the experiences her students cocreate with her are always better than anything she could devise on her own.

Map the Journey

Before we complete an experience and let it out into the wild, we use one final tool that we call mapping the journey. First we design what we think of as an entrance into the experience. The goals at this point are to introduce the red thread, make a safe

CENTER
Activate the senses
Cocreate
Stir surprise and suspense

ENTRANCE
Introduce a red thread
Make a safe space
Spark wonder

EXIT
Close open ends
Reflect on experience
Let one question linger

space that invites exploration, and spark wonder. If the experience is a presentation, the entrance may be a question or a story. If the experience is a gift, the entrance may be an invitation to find it.

The heart of the experience is the center. This segment is where you activate the senses and cocreate the experience with participants. The center is the place to unfold your surprises little by little, stringing them together with suspense and meaning. The best centers have unexpected twists and turns while letting participants know that they are still headed in the right direction. In a presentation, the center houses conversations, exercises, and demonstrations. In a gift-giving experience, the center is where the gift is unveiled, ideally only one small portion at a time.

Finally, you reach the exit: the conclusion of the journey. At this point, the Find Phase of the Surprise Sequence should draw to an end by wrapping up loose ends. The Shift and Share Phases can also happen thanks to some reflection on what everyone just felt and learned. Ideally though, a hint of the wonder sparked throughout the experience is left to linger. An exit for a presentation may be a summary and a chance for participants to share their insights. The exit for a gift-giving experience may be a final message from the gift giver or the opportunity to use the gift.

The idea of a journey also applies to experiences you design for yourself. Most people are great at creating the center of an experience, but they generally forget the entrance and exit. Next time you go to a party, take a moment to ask yourself what you hope to get out of the experience and what you are curious to learn. Once it's time to leave, instead of opening your email and shifting your attention to something new, reflect on what you experienced. Shifting our attention immediately after an experience ends can lead us to forget much of what just happened. A disruption prevents information in our short-term memories from moving into our long-term memories, where we can have continuous access to it. In a world of countless stimuli vying for our attention, we risk missing the full impact of our experiences by shifting focus too soon. Ending experiences by reflecting and letting some wonder linger allows our experiences to stay with us forever.

Have you noticed that we've mapped the journey throughout this chapter? That means that we've now reached the exit and need to tie up loose ends and leave a question to linger. In short, the more surprise something holds, the more it is an experience. Experiences plug us into the moment, connect us with people and the world, and imbue objects and events with value—making even the driest turkey (or Tofurkey) delicious. To engineer the unexpected through experience making, create a red thread, activate the senses, cocreate, and map the journey. The only question left is, *What experience will you design next?*

··· CHEAT SHEET ···

CHAPTER NINE

THE BITE-SIZE VERSION

The difference between a commodity, service, and experience is in the amount of surprise you feel when interacting with it. More surprise makes things more experiential. Experiences are immersive, memorable, and transformative.

TOOLS

- **Create a red thread:** unite the elements of your experience with a single theme or recurring message.
- **Activate the senses:** enhance your experiences by exciting each of the senses (especially the ones that tend to get overlooked).
- **Cocreate:** invite participants to help make the experience with you. Leave negative space so that others can fill it.
- **Map the journey:** create an entrance, center, and exit for your experience. Start by creating safety and sparking wonder. End by tying up loose ends, allowing time for reflection, and leaving a question to linger.

EXERCISE YOUR SURPRISE MUSCLE

It's time to embrace your destiny as an experience maker. Pick someone to invite over for dinner next week. Now start plotting. How can you turn the event into an experience (a good experience)?

PART FOUR

Everyday SURPRISE

*I wake up with the hope this day is even
more uncertain than yesterday . . .
If a life can be a series of perpetual surprises,
that's the most joyous experience you
can have.*

—DEEPAK CHOPRA

Dearest Reader,

*It is a sad truth we all have to accept. Most diets don't work for
long. Most advice doesn't stick. Most inspiration doesn't last. Making sustainable changes in our lives takes constant effort. And we
humans like to conserve our energy. We have evolved to be lazy.
We all slip into unintentional living from time to time (even trained
Surprisologists). The best way to combat this quirk of human nature is to harness the power of habit.*

*In the final section of the book, we invite you to think about
how you can embrace and engineer surprise as part of everyday*

life. How can you make surprise a habit rather than an occasional treat for your brain?

The most meaningful places to practice everyday surprise are our relationships and our way of life. When we apply skillful surprise to ourselves and our interactions with others, connection, excitement, and fulfillment become an everyday occurrence too. In these final two chapters we'll explore how to cultivate relationships through surprise and how to surprise ourselves every single day.

See you in the deep end!
Your fellow Surprisologists

Chapter Ten

Cultivate Relationships

In the span of eighty years, Jean and Dina saw many changes. They finished school, fell in love with the men they went on to marry, lived in a total of sixteen states with their respective families, and watched their children grow into adulthood. But one thing has remained unchanged. They have been best friends since they first met at the age of seven in 1934. Distance and the busyness of life prevented them from seeing one another often, but they never lost touch. They mailed letters and gifts. They visited whenever possible. They called often—sharing secrets, fears, and laughter over the phone like teenagers even in their eighties. And they supported one another through the toughest moments of their lives. Seeing the women together is awe-inspiring. They beam with joy and share glances that contain eight decades of memories. Jean and Dina don't just maintain their relationship. They cultivate it.

The quality of our relationships impacts the quality of our

lives. We, Tania and LeeAnn, know this well thanks to the depth of our own friendship and professional partnership. If it weren't for our friendship, this book wouldn't exist (and our lives wouldn't be nearly as wonderful). Cultivating relationships is one of the biggest investments any of us can make in our emotional and physical well-being. Our friends, coworkers, clients, romantic partners, family members, and neighbors all contribute to our perception of ourselves and of the world. Harmful relationships can lead to heartache, fear, wariness, and frustration. Rewarding relationships lead to resilience, inspiration, growth, and fulfillment. As with most things in life, if we aren't intentional in cultivating our relationships, we find ourselves surrounded by more weeds than flowers.

EVERYDAY RELATIONSHIP TOOLS

You don't need to wait eighty years for your relationships to blossom. Relationships thrive from a skillful application of surprise. Not just every once in a while but every day. In this chapter, we'll share six surprise-based tools for cultivating relationships: maintain complexity, balance oneness and otherness, balance novelty and routine, practice the magic ratio, speak the right surprise language, and track patterns. Though each dynamic is different, you'll find that surprise plays a similar role in every kind of relationship.

Maintain Complexity

A sea of people sways in the darkness, voices brittle from screaming. Green and yellow searchlights slide across the audience, illuminating fists pumping, hands thrusting toward the stage in the sign of the horns, and heads thrashing. Nearly everyone is dressed in black and covered in piercings. From a distance, it looks like any heavy-metal concert, but if you listen closely, you'll notice something unusual. On stage, a man grips the microphone with both hands and sings: "Evil falls on each of us, there's nothing new. Who cares if you're a Muslim or a Jew? The awakened ones are nothing but a few. And the one to make the difference now is you." Look more closely, and you'll see something else unexpected: Christians, Muslims, and Jews standing side by side in the audience and shouting the lyrics together.

This scene is typical at an Orphaned Land concert—an Israeli band that blends Euro-American metal with traditional Middle Eastern sounds, instruments, and religious texts. They make a point of expressing their love for their Jewish and Muslim fans. On the band's fan forum and Facebook page there are no vicious debates over politics or religion—only heated conversation about music and, sometimes, a passion for peace. All over the world, fans from traditionally fragmented areas (Israel, Jordan, Egypt, Palestine, Turkey, Iran) come together to enjoy Orphaned Land concerts. Individuals who may have hated one another in a different context become best friends.

Orphaned Land fans practice one of the most important tools for cultivating relationships. They maintain complexity.

Instead of protecting their schemata around culture and religion, they let surprise in. Through the relationships they form with their supposed enemies, they learn to think "I don't like this person's beliefs" and "This is a good person" at the same time. It is a challenging skill to master—especially in moments of conflict when we protect our schemata—but when we maintain complexity and let surprise into our thinking about all our relationships, we give them the opportunity to thrive.

Conflict scholar Roi Ben-Yehuda told us, "What the research has shown is that complexity matters. The good news is that people who are able to maintain nuanced—even contradictory—narratives of their life situations report greater satisfaction in dealing with conflicts, having more tolerance for others, and maintaining healthier relationships. The bad news is that during times of particularly difficult conflicts there is a tendency for complexity to collapse. This exacerbates destructive conflicts. It is therefore essential for us to figure out ways to increase and foster complexity in our lives." Researchers at Columbia University's Conflict Lab have found that the most persistent conflicts are those that participants perceive as simple and surprise free when they are actually extraordinarily complex. *I'm right, and you're wrong; We're good, and they're evil; You're the instigator, and I'm the victim*—these are all unambiguous ways to think of conflict that feel comfortable to our brains but only make the conflict worse.

Conflict presents the biggest danger *and* opportunity for relationships. When bad surprises strike, individuals who can't maintain complexity shift their perspective about one another and decide that the relationship can't work. But by maintaining complexity and staying open to surprise, we can flex and use conflict to deepen our relationships. Not only does conflict allow us to broaden our perspectives, it also gives us a chance to show others that we accept them for who they really are. As Jean said in an interview about her best friend, Dina, "We can share everything with each other and still be all right. You can't do that with too many people."[1]

To maintain complexity in your relationships, stop whenever you notice that you're thinking of someone in simplistic terms. That includes overly positive perceptions like "He's perfect," and "She's brilliant." When we hear a new employee say that his boss is perfect, we know it's a red flag; he's setting himself up for an unpleasant surprise. Rose-tinted glasses may be pleasant, but clear lenses are best for cultivating lasting relationships. Notice and accept the complex and surprisingly contradictory qualities of the people in your life and even within yourself. Flash Rosenberg takes award-winning photos and is artist-in-residence at the New York Public Library, but when describing herself she tells us, "I've never thought of myself as an 'er' or an 'ist'—an artist, performer, photographer—I am just curious about many different things."

Another way to maintain complexity is to zoom out and search for context. Our brains understand that there are many reasons for our *own* actions, but they tend to assume that the reason for other people's actions is only their personalities. This tendency is called the fundamental attribution error. If someone smiles, we think she's nice. If someone snaps at us, we assume she's rude. Instead of following this instinct, we can get in the habit of asking, *What else is leading to this person's behavior?* Could it be that when someone is rude she's just having a bad day?

In *The Five Percent,* a book on particularly stubborn conflict, Peter Coleman (director of the International Center for Cooperation and Conflict Resolution at Columbia University) points out that maintaining complexity is important for most systems.[2] For example, the heart shifts from a complex to a simple pattern right before cardiac arrest. In the same way, relationships that embrace surprise by inviting complexity in roles and perspectives tend to be the healthiest (and most fulfilling).

Balance Oneness and Otherness

Caitlin and Kara have been together for fourteen years. When they first started dating, it felt like there was never enough time to discover all the little details of one another's lives. "I couldn't stand the thought of not knowing something about her," Caitlin told us. "It's like I had to hold on to that shovel and just keep digging." Caitlin and Kara were enmeshed in the Find Phase of the Surprise Sequence for several months. Soon their perseverance paid off—but not as they hoped: "Now she'll start telling me a story, and I'm like 'I know, I know, I've heard that one already.'"

Like most couples, Caitlin and Kara began their courtship with an overwhelming desire to reduce their *otherness* and increase their *oneness.* In other words, they wanted to find ways to close the distance between them and feel as connected as possible. Today they can predict one another's words, actions, and facial expressions, and their friends say they are even starting to look alike. Thanks to the almost complete lack of surprise in their relationship, Caitlin and Kara are secure and comfortable, but they are missing the passion that comes with otherness—the excitement and allure of surprise.

Though balancing oneness and otherness applies to all types of relationships, it poses an even greater challenge in the case of romantic partnership. The more our partners feel like family, the more we trust them. The more they feel like strangers, the more we want them. This tension is the ultimate romantic enigma. We are drawn to our partners because they harbor secrets and surprises, but once we've unlocked the secrets and our partners can no longer surprise us, we lose interest. From a neurochemical perspective, this irony is likely caused by a dance between dopamine and oxytocin. Dopamine is linked with desire, and oxytocin is called the "cuddle chemical." As oxytocin levels go up, dopamine levels take a nose dive.[3] Despite these opposing forces, most of us want to have predictability *and* surprise, dopamine *and* oxytocin, oneness *and* otherness, all rolled into just one relationship.

Psychologist Esther Perel calls this phenomenon a crisis of desire.[4] She has interviewed people from more than twenty countries and found the same phenomenon across the world. Individuals crave stability and oneness, but they report being most drawn to their partners when there is distance between them. The distance can be physical—like when you spend time apart—or it can be mental, like when our partners manage to surprise us or show us a side of themselves that we don't usually see.

Simply watching our partners from a distance, especially

when they are in their element and at their best, could do the trick. In Esther's words, desire is triggered when "this person that is already so familiar, so known, is momentarily once again somewhat mysterious, somewhat elusive."[5] She says the most attractive quality in a partner is radiant confidence—the sense that this individual is totally self-sustaining and has a rich and separate inner world.

Too much distance is not ideal either. To feel playful, mischievous, and confident, we also need to feel safe and accepted. To take the kinds of risks that make us attractive to our partners, we need to believe that they won't lose respect for us when we step into new and unknown territory. The key is to find a balance between oneness and otherness so that there is just the right amount of surprise and predictability.

The need for balance is most obvious in romantic partnerships, but balancing oneness and otherness is vital for all relationships. Think back to childhood best friends Jean and Dina. They share their innermost thoughts, but they also lead separate lives. This balance fosters a relationship that is both comforting and invigorating. In our work, we see the same dynamic between coworkers: if they remain too distant, trust and collaboration suffer. If they share too much, productivity and innovation plummet. Even in families, too much involvement in one another's lives can lead to frustration, while too little can lead to isolation.

Take a look at the diagrams below representing relationships between two people. Dyad A is so close that there is more shared than separate between them—more one than other. The result is lots of security and little excitement. Dyad B is at the other end of the spectrum. There might be excitement but not enough comfort and safety. Dyad C gets the Goldilocks prize for having just the right balance on the Surprise See-saw. Of course, relationships aren't always symmetrical. In some cases, person 1 may know everything about person 2, but person 2 is a mystery. Person 1 feels insecure, while person 2 feels bored. Person 1 needs less surprise. Person 2 needs more.

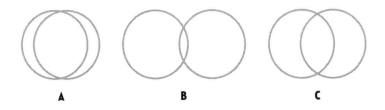

A   B   C

In relationships like Caitlin and Kara's (exhibit A), finding that elusive equilibrium requires developing individual identity rather than shared identity. We like to think of it as making deposits in two different accounts: the One and the Other. To grow the One account, individuals can collect shared experiences and give each other access to their private thoughts and feelings. To invest in the Other account, they can seek out separate projects, hobbies, friends, and experiences. The goal isn't to move farther apart, but to constantly grow the Other account so that there are always enough funds to spark mystery and produce surprise.

Another way to spot the surprising side of the people in your life is to stay curious and assume that there is always more to discover. Sue, who described her relationship with Dave as "stale pizza" or "an EKG machine flat-lining," learned this lesson accidentally while shopping for Christmas gifts at Macy's. Her friend was rummaging through a stack of sweaters when she casually asked Sue what Dave's favorite color was. Sue was about to say green because she always bought him green clothes, but just then it occurred to her that she wasn't so sure. That night as they sat on the couch watching a Yankees' game, Sue asked Dave about his favorite color and was shocked to learn that it was blue. Dave asked if Sue's favorite color was green. "No, why?" she asked. "Well, you're always buying me green clothes," he answered. "At that moment, a lightbulb went off in my head," Sue told us. "I started to wonder how many other things we just presumed about each other, and it hit me that you have to stay curious." We typically don't think about balancing oneness and otherness until we find that our relationships are bringing us less joy. Before trouble starts brewing in paradise, think about how you can make deposits into your One and Other accounts every day, little by little.

Balance Novelty and Routine

Thirty years ago, a group of friends created a gourmet club. Every year since, they have been getting together around a dining room table to eat good food.[6] Club members have to live by a few important rules: Take turns hosting the dinner parties, make time for them (even when life threatens to get in the way), and bring your dish no matter how it turns out. Each gathering has a theme, from "all things Idaho" to "Greek cooking for the gods." Sometimes the culinary concoctions are a success and sometimes they're a total failure. As time passes, the friends grow closer and manage to have even more fun together.

The gourmet club exemplifies a concept that is closely related to oneness and otherness. It strikes a balance between novelty and routine. Novelty triggers surprise. It gives us an experience we couldn't have expected because we've never had it before. Too little routine means too much surprise, which produces relationships that are unstable. Too little novelty means not enough surprise, which dooms relationships to dullness.

In one set of experiments, researchers examined whether simply spending time together as a couple is enough or if novelty is necessary to keep the sparks flying.[7] They asked some couples to share experiences that they considered pleasant (visiting friends, going to church). They asked other couples to share experiences that the partners considered new and exciting (going skiing, attending a concert). Sharing novel, surprise-inducing activities increased relationship satisfaction significantly more than simply sharing pleasant experiences. But just to be sure that they stumbled on a meaningful finding, the researchers got more creative.

They placed mats around a large room and set up a barrier in the center. Next they bound couples together with Velcro straps and told them to travel from mat to mat across the barrier on their hands and knees while carrying a pillow without using their hands, arms, or teeth in under one minute (true story). For another group of couples, the researchers set up a less surprising activity. One partner had to roll a ball to the center of the room while the other slowly retrieved it on all fours. It turned out that only the surprising, novel activity boosted relationship satisfaction. In short, spending time together is important, but it isn't enough. The trick is to share pleasant, routine experiences and mix in surprises too.

All types of relationships benefit from a balance of novelty and familiarity. In our workshops, we often ask participants to describe their most fulfilling relationships. To our delight, many of them talk about the relationships they've forged with their clients. Routine meetings and calls create security, and novel experiences (from impromptu tandem bike rides to sharing unusual meals) trigger surprise and excitement. Take a moment to think about your relationships. Which of them feel too insecure or unreliable? Which feel too stale and predictable? What can you do to find a balance?

Practice the Magic Ratio

Psychologist John Gottman is very good at predicting whether a married couple will stay together. He's so good at it that he often jokes that it's the reason he doesn't get invited to more dinner parties. John has predicted divorce with about 94 percent accuracy in 677 couples.[8] He says it's really pretty simple. One of the easiest ways to predict whether a couple will break up is to look at their ratio of negative to positive actions. He discovered that couples who split up tend to have more negative interactions (such as criticizing, lying, avoiding) than positive ones (such as listening, helping, touching). The most stable couples don't simply have a balance between negative and positive experiences (I came home late, so I got you a present), they have what John calls the magic ratio: five positive experiences for every one negative experience.[9] Though researchers debate over just how many positives we need to outweigh the negatives, the general concept of the magic ratio appears across all sorts of relationships—from the personal to the professional. We need more positives than negatives.

We humans have evolved to treat negative experiences as stronger currency than the positive ones. This reality is important to keep in mind when we think back to the Shift Phase of the Surprise Sequence. Our brains are constantly constructing and maintaining schemata. Surprise forces us to stop and examine whether we need to make adjustments to these schemata or fortify them even more. The magic ratio reveals that one unpleasant surprise creates a more intense schema shift than one pleasant surprise. It also means that a positive surprise won't always create an immediate shift but a gradual transition. If your positive surprise deposits don't seem to be paying off, stay patient and remember that shift happens (but only after our schemata have collected enough evidence to change).

In our work with teams that can't seem to build strong relationships, we find that practicing the magic ratio can create a meaningful shift. We ask team members to consider how many positive and negative surprises they've gotten and given recently. If their ratio is off (and it nearly always is), we have them create a plan for engineering more delight and communicating their needs more clearly to help prevent disappointment.

If you have inadvertently given someone a negative surprise lately, it will cost you approximately five positive surprises to get out of the red. To strengthen our relationships every day, we can make positive deposits into people's schema accounts regularly so that when bad surprises surface, our relationships are strong enough to handle them.

Speak the Right Surprise Language

Hao prided himself on being a great father. His two sons looked up to him, trusted him, and enjoyed spending time with him—even when they grew into teenagers. When his third son, Alan, was born, he thought: "Piece of cake." But by the time Alan was six years old, it was clear that his relationship with his father was different. No matter how hard Hao tried, he couldn't seem to bond with his son. As Alan grew older, their relationship grew more distant. Most attempts Hao made to connect with his son seemed to end in disappointment. Hao tried to surprise him with new clothes, toys, and spontaneous trips. But each time, Alan reacted to the surprises as though he were hurt. The relationship was baffling. Hao fought to keep an open mind and craft a balance between excitement and stability. He made sure to limit negative surprises and devise plenty of positive ones. But he was missing one more piece of the relationship puzzle: speaking the right surprise language. This tool is based on a theory by theologian and relationship counselor Gary Chapman, author of *The Five Love Languages*.[10]

According to Gary, at the core of most relationship problems is a mismatch between how individuals "speak" love. After conducting hundreds of interviews, Gary came to the conclusion that there are five distinct love languages: physical touch (like hugging), words of affirmation (such as giving compliments), quality time (sharing experiences or having deep conversations), acts of service (for example, helping with chores), and gifts (including tangible and intangible items). He noticed that individuals often feel unloved or unappreciated simply because people aren't speaking their primary love language. He saw the same pattern in families, couples, and professional relationships.

After learning about the love language theory, we realized this idea applies perfectly to surprise. Now, before we devise a surprise for people, we first take the time to understand which love language they speak. If your boss is most moved by words, even the most elaborate gift won't make an impact, but a simple, handwritten card will make her day. If your mother cares most about sharing quality time, surprising her with a poem about how wonderful she is won't mean as much to her as a surprise day out with you (even if you do manage to find the perfect rhyme for *mom*).

Think back to our discussion about delight. It's not enough to simply exceed expectations. What matters most is exceeding the most important expectations, speaking the *right* surprise language. To do this in any relationship, we need to be aware of what others are expecting (and hoping). Often, the answer to this question is counterintuitive.

In Hao and Alan's relationship, a shift finally happened once Hao started paying attention to how Alan expressed his love. He noticed that unlike his older sons, Alan always said, "I love you," before going to bed or leaving the house. Hao would pat him on the back or nod, but he found it difficult to say the words back. Just the thought of it made him uncomfortable and awkward. It wasn't how he was raised.

One night, Hao decided to change the surprise language he had been using with his son. He had tried to give him gifts and plan exciting activities, but his efforts never paid off. Hao took out a sheet of paper and pen. He placed them on the table and stared at them for a long time. Eventually he picked up the pen and wrote, "I'm proud of you. Love, Dad." He taped the note to his son's door and went to sleep. Alan didn't mention the note the next morning, but when he saw his father, he smiled. They ate breakfast together for the first time in years. Hao had uncovered his son's love language, and now he knew which surprises would be most meaningful.

What is your love language? What kinds of surprises make you happiest? What surprises would be most meaningful to the people in your life? Don't save them for special occasions. Small surprises sprinkled into a relationship often are far more meaningful than big but rare surprises. If you aren't sure of the right language to use, pay attention to the surprises people create for you and the ways in which they express their love and appreciation. We typically give love in the ways that we hope to receive it. If that doesn't work, it can't hurt to experiment.

Track Patterns

By the time Rex met Geraldine he had long been set in his ways—distrustful, solitary, and often aggressive. Geraldine was no picnic either, described by others as cranky and destructive. But when the two met, something changed in Rex. Not only was he loving and patient with Geraldine, he also became friendlier with everyone else. The transformation was remarkable. What makes this story even more unusual is that Rex is a German shepherd and Geraldine is a goose. The pair lives at the Puriton Horse and Animal Rescue in Somerset, England. They have breakfast together, go on long walks through the woods, and even sleep in the same dog bed every night. Rex and Geraldine's friendship is unusual but the sudden shift in Rex's relationship with his human handlers (from vicious to mellow) is not. Geraldine's appearance at the animal rescue was a surprise—it interrupted his patterns, which led an entirely new set of behaviors to emerge in his relationships.

Our final and favorite tool for cultivating relationships is tracking patterns. The good, the bad, and the boring. Our patterns are the behaviors that contain no surprise. They are predictable, so we are usually blind to them. When we track our patterns, a whole world of possibility opens. Think of the patterns in your relationships. When you have a meeting with your coworker, what makes him happiest? What gets him frustrated? When you visit your family, what do you fight about? What do you bond over? If you aren't sure, pay attention. When you find yourself in the midst of a pleasant or unpleasant situation in your relationships, pause and ask what triggered it.

Don't forget that you are part of the pattern. Particularly in moments of conflict, we tend to notice what others are doing to make the situation worse, but we don't see our role in perpetuating the conflict. Even though Tania knows this principle well, she still occasionally falls into the pattern trap in her relationship with her sister, Kat. (Some patterns are stickier than others.) When they fight, Tania inevitably believes that she is the innocent victim and her sister, the stubborn perpetrator. A typical exchange goes like this:

> KAT: You should put on gloves.
> TANIA: I'm okay. Thanks.
> KAT: But it's cold.
> TANIA: But I'm not cold.
> KAT: Here, take my gloves.
> TANIA: I don't want your gloves!
> KAT: Why won't you take them?
> TANIA: Because I'm not cold!

Beneath this baffling exchange, there are hidden patterns that stem from their long history of sisterhood. Kat feels hurt because Tania won't let her help. Tania feels hurt because Kat is stepping on her autonomy. Only when Tania stops long enough to detect the pattern can she zoom out and realize that she is also contributing to the situation. She can stop the glove wars by simply expressing her gratitude for her sister's concern. (Yes, Kat, you have the confession here in writing.)

When we track our patterns we understand how our behaviors affect our relationships. We can also spot patterns that lead to our best experiences together. Once we know what these patterns are, we can replicate them. As marriage counselor Michele Weiner-Davis puts it, we can "do more of what works, less of what doesn't."[11] And last, when we spot patterns that we don't like, we can mix in surprise and interrupt them.

Think back to the relationship between Rex and Geraldine.

Meeting each other interrupted their daily routines and long-held habits. They couldn't keep doing the same things in the same way because there was now something new in the system. You can interrupt patterns in your relationships simply by doing something you don't typically do. Instead of getting defensive, thank your sister for her glove offering and maybe even give her a hug. Instead of holding predictably boring meetings with your employees, arrange a picnic and move your conversation outside. *How* you interrupt the pattern matters less than *that* you interrupt the pattern. Try different surprises and keep using the ones that work.

Our relationships thrive when we spend every day cultivating them. For example, today. Which of your relationships most needs your attention? How can you apply surprise to this relationship in one small way?

THE BITE-SIZE VERSION

The quality of our relationships determines the quality of our lives. Cultivate your relationships every day. (Today included.) Relationships thrive from a balance of predictability and surprise.

TOOLS

- **Maintain complexity:** hold opposing views at the same time about yourself and others.
- **Balance oneness with otherness:** find a balance between what you know and don't know to create comfort *and* intrigue.
- **Balance novelty and routine:** combine exciting new experiences with tradition.
- **Practice the magic ratio:** notice the ratio of positive to negative experiences in your relationships. Be sure you are engineering more positive than negative surprises.
- **Speak the right surprise language:** discover people's love languages (words, touch, gifts, quality time, or service). Surprise them in the ways they find most meaningful.
- **Track patterns:** spot routine behaviors. Do more of what works and less of what doesn't. To spark change, interrupt patterns you don't like.

EXERCISE YOUR SURPRISE MUSCLE

Your friend is having trouble in his relationship of fifteen years. That's a long time! He says it no longer feels fulfilling. They've run out of things to talk about and just sit around watching TV on the weekends. He knows you are a phenomenal advice giver, so he turns to you for help. What do you recommend?

. . . .

Chapter Eleven

Surprise Yourself

Tania thinks of herself as a happy person. Her friends make fun of her because she compulsively points out the silver lining in the worst situations ("But on the bright side . . ."). She rarely gets upset. She laughs a lot. Her face is often sore at the end of the day from smiling. So a little while back, it was startling for her to recognize that she had gotten depressed. It wasn't that she was upset about anything. It was more that her days lost their flavor. Nothing seemed enjoyable. Nothing seemed interesting.

It started off with some bad news followed by a few gloomy days. She waited to snap out of it, but the feeling stuck around like a friend who crashes on your couch past the point of welcome. Days stretched into weeks. When getting out of bed still felt like a waste of time over a month later, she realized she had to make some changes. Tania had experienced full-blown depression as a teenager, and she wasn't willing to let that feeling return. Not when she knew that life could be so good.

She mustered enough energy to survey her life in search of the problem. She couldn't find one. On the contrary. She loved her work and felt deep connection in her relationships. Why wouldn't that awful, muted sadness go away? She looked closer. Instead of examining her life as a whole, she turned her attention to her days. Every day. That's where she spotted the problem. Her days had become routine and predictable. She was running a company called Surprise Industries, for crying out loud, but she wasn't surprising *herself*.

EVERYDAY SURPRISE TOOLS

Life can surprise us. People can surprise us. We can surprise people. But how can we possibly surprise ourselves? Most people assume it's impossible. But it's not just possible to surprise ourselves, it's vital. Not only when we're stuck or sad but in our day-to-day lives. When we're surprised, we're completely present, wildly curious, expanding our perspectives, and connected with others. In other words, when we're surprised we are more deeply connected and thoroughly alive. Not too shabby for one funny-looking little emotion. Sometimes life supplies us with all the surprise we need, but usually it's up to us to weave surprise into each day. In this final chapter, we'll show you five ways to surprise yourself: collect novelty, turn on wonder, seek awe, grow your comfort zone, and practice gratitude.

Collect Novelty

One of the first steps Tania took toward shaking off her depression was collecting novelty. That week, she took a new dance class, bought a new book, saw a new show, and scheduled meetings with two new people. From a psychological standpoint, novelty is simply an experience you've never had before. It surprises us because we don't know what to expect from it or what feelings and behaviors it will trigger.

When researchers used a functional MRI to track participants' brain reactions to novelty, they learned two things.[1] First, novel stimuli (in the form of new pictures) capture attention more than familiar and even preferred stimuli (such as the participants' favorite pictures). Second, the brain processes novel information in a completely different way from information it has already seen—even if it has seen it just once before. Only completely novel stimuli activate the midbrain and release dopamine.

Aside from activating dopamine (which triggers the Find Phase of the Surprise Sequence), novelty also sparks the Shift Phase. It creates new synaptic pathways in the brain—almost like an explorer traversing uncharted grounds. The more unique and surprising the experience, the more unique the synaptic pathway. Like Robert Frost's road less traveled . . . on a neural level. These new pathways create behavioral flexibility and spark new emotions and ideas. Novelty can get us unstuck and take us to new places.

If doing something new feels scary or uncomfortable, consider the advice of Chris Guillebeau, author of *The Art of*

Nonconformity. He told us in an interview, "You gather the courage to try new things by trying new things . . . and then realizing that not only did you not have anything to be afraid of but new things are usually fun and meaningful. They don't always have to be big things—just taking a walk or going somewhere new for lunch is a good start."

Turn on Wonder

What made Wonderland so different from Alice's reality? You can point to the disappearing cat, the talking caterpillar, or Alice's persistent shape shifting, but there are countless fascinating and surprising things in the real world too. The true difference between Alice's two worlds is that in Wonderland she wondered. She stayed within the Find Phase of the Surprise Sequence without seeking to bring it to a close. Back in her regular life, she wasn't nearly as open. The lesson from Alice's journey is that the very act of wondering changes our experience. Surprise triggers wonder, as in the case of white rabbits with gold watches, but the equation works in both directions. When we turn on wonder, we spot surprise.

In Chapter 6, we shared a creativity tool called get to curious. Curiosity and wonder both happen in the Find Phase of the Surprise Sequence. But is there a subtle difference between them? Take a moment to feel curious. Now feel wonder. Most people make this distinction: While curiosity pushes us to look for answers, wonder allows us to savor the questions. Curiosity is focused. Wonder is open. As far as we know, wonder never killed the cat.

To turn on wonder, slow down and look closer. In one of his many notebooks, Leonardo da Vinci wrote: "If you look at walls that are stained or made of different kinds of stones you can think you see in them certain picturesque views of mountains, rivers, rocks, trees, plains, broad valleys, and hills of different shapes. You can also find in them battles and rapidly moving figures, strange faces and costumes, as well as an infinite number of things."[2] Imagine feeling as much wonder as da Vinci about everything around you—things, places, animals, plants, people, and especially yourself.

In Tania's case, collecting novelty drew her away from her slump, but wonder brought her over the edge. She went on a stroll through the park, actively turned on wonder, and looked at the world with fresh eyes. In her mind, she held a single thought: "I wonder what I will see." It was a windy world, with leaves rushing across streets and colorful scarves blowing behind people like capes. Tania walked slowly, breathing in the scents in the air, running her fingers across plants and fences, and listening carefully. A gust of wind swept in from the water, and she

spotted her shadow on a tree. Her hair was standing straight up like a flame or one of those troll dolls from the 1960s. The sight triggered the first genuine smile she had all month.

Psychologist Todd Kashdan points out that small surprises lie even in the most familiar areas of our lives: "No two hugs are the same, no two pizzerias make pizza slices the same way, no two times we watch *The Godfather* are the same, and so it goes."[3] With every passing second our world changes a little and we change along with it. If the change isn't surprising enough, our brains don't bother calling our attention to it. But when we turn on wonder, small surprises instantly appear.

Researchers Timothy Wilson and Dan Gilbert decided to test the effects of wonder.[4] They had participants watch a movie while reading one of two scripts out loud. One group of participants read: "I see. That makes sense. Of course." The other group read: "I wonder. Huh? I don't get it." The researchers then asked participants how much they liked the film and what emotions they experienced. People who read the wonder phrases liked the film more and experienced significantly more positive emotion than the people who read the certain phrases. The researchers' conclusion? Wondering makes life more enjoyable.

Seek Awe

Imagine the feeling you get staring up at a night sky that's shimmering with shooting stars, glancing into the heart of a volcano, standing in a darkened field aglow with thousands of fireflies, or hearing a swell of hundreds of violins. It's an emotion on the surprise spectrum called awe. As in the true meaning of awesome. Awe is surprise that's stirred by something unfathomably vast or complex. We can't quite believe it even as we stand before it. Nature is the most common awe trigger, but intricate design, extraordinary skill, admirable integrity, and remarkable ideas also inspire awe. Like all surprises, awe leads us to stop, wonder, shift our perspective, and long to share our experiences with others (which explains why tourists are always snapping photos). But the Shift Phase in instances of awe is unique.

Awe leads us to reframe ourselves as small and our world as vast. Researchers have found that simply watching awe-inspiring nature videos created this shift and also led participants to feel like they had more time.[5] Psychologists have nicknamed this time-stretching phenomenon "extended-now"—when now feels longer than the usual fragment of a moment. Awe also led participants to be more patient and helpful. Helping increases happiness, so awe doesn't just feel awesome but also improves our quality of life.[6]

We have to actively seek awe because it is a rare emotion. Whenever you can, surround yourself with nature, beauty, and inspiring people and ideas. As a citizen of our time-starved world, you might occasionally feel that you can't step away from your daily hassles long enough to let in awe, but it can also work the other way around. Experience awe and, suddenly, you will feel that you have all the time in the world.

Grow Your Comfort Zone

One of our first clients at Surprise Industries was a soft-spoken nutritionist from Brooklyn named Kavita. Over the phone she explained that she wanted a surprise for her husband, Hamel, to help him face his slight fear of heights. The surprise team exchanged a nervous glance, gulped, and got to work selecting an experience for unsuspecting Hamel.

Two weeks later, Kavita and Hamel showed up at an un-marked building behind a winding alley with no idea what would happen. Well, that's not entirely accurate. Kavita had *some* idea what would happen. She expected to see her husband squirm and sweat as she patted him on the back and squeezed his hand with encouragement. She was wrong.

Of course, we can't reveal the surprise we arranged for the couple, but we can tell you that it took Kavita and Hamel sev-eral stories off the ground. To everyone's amazement, Hamel was ecstatic. He wore a huge grin the whole time and said he may have found a new life calling. Kavita's reaction was equally unexpected. She was terrified. Actually, she was so terrified that she is still the only person in the history of Surprise Indus-tries to throw up at a surprise. We were hesitant to ask for feed-back. After all, we thought, she puked. Nobody likes to puke. But Kavita surprised us again. She said that it had been one of the best experiences of her life.

Kavita's story is no longer unusual to us—but it still sounds counterintuitive. How can doing something that feels so wrong be so right? We humans work incredibly hard to have comfort and predictability in our lives, but it's those moments in which we surprise ourselves and grow our comfort zone that we find the most meaningful. In Kavita's story we see the same strange paradox of human nature that LeeAnn stumbled across long ago in her research on authentic happiness: We feel most com-fortable when things are certain, but we feel most alive when they're not.

Step outside your comfort zone. You've probably heard it said so often that it has lost all meaning (and maybe even taken on that distinct scent of cheesiness). But for us, this saying took on new freshness when we saw it through the lens of surprise. Neurologically speaking, our comfort zone is our realm of certainty. It is a place where no surprises dwell, which makes us feel calm and in control. Outside the imaginary line of this zone is the unknown—a land that's rich with surprise. Stepping outside your comfort zone invites in surprise, and you already know by now why that's exhilarating. But there's more to it than that. When you take one small step outside that realm of certainty, you aren't just going out on your own, you are dragging that imaginary boundary between you and the great unknown along with you. By stepping outside your comfort zone you actually grow your comfort zone.

Your brain sorts information into two categories: novel and familiar. Experiencing something new just once immediately makes it old. So while taking one flamenco class will not make you instantly comfortable dancing flamenco, no class will ever be as uncomfortable again as the first.

As proponents of a well-balanced Surprise Seesaw, we do not recommend that you spend all your time leaping far outside your comfort zone or even marching out of it steadily. Sometimes safety and stability are important, and our comfort zone is the coziest spot in the world. We all need to snuggle with our security blankets from time to time. But it is important to distinguish whether we are choosing to stay inside our comfort zones or our comfort zones are keeping us captive. Nurture the things in your life that are safe and certain, especially your relationships and your values. But once you have stable ground, if you find that stepping outside your comfort zone is still too painful, then you have a good indicator that it's time to do exactly that. Just as our muscles ache when they are growing and stretching, so does our very sense of self when we grow as individuals.

For added impetus, think about regret. In a study, participants were asked to rate what they regretted more in the past week: action or inaction (such as doing nothing when they wanted to do something).[7] While 53 percent of participants reported regretting actions, 47 percent regretted inaction. But here's the twist: With time, regrets of action fade away and often transform into pride. Regrets of inaction linger and grow. When looking over their lives as a whole, 16 percent of participants said they regretted action. A whopping 84 percent said they regretted inaction most. Growing our comfort zones inch by inch every day allows us to travel miles over time and feel joy when we think back on where we've been and how far we've come.

Practice Gratitude

What makes you feel grateful? How often do you feel gratitude? One of the best predictors of life satisfaction is how much gratitude we feel on a regular basis.[8] More gratitude = more joy. Easier said than done. Remember the expectation bar? As soon as something delights us, the bar rises. If our newly elevated standards continue to be met, the bar settles in and gets comfy where it is. When we get what we expect (even if it's wonderful), we feel nothing. No surprise = no gratitude. Actively practicing gratitude is the only way to flip on the switch voluntarily instead of sitting around and waiting for gratitude-inspiring surprise to happen.

We can reset our expectation bars by seeking out examples of situations that we would find disappointing and yet are perfectly normal by other people's standards. A fresh perspective resets our expectation bars and allows us to be pleasantly surprised again. We can also harness the power of random reinforcement and treat ourselves to luxuries only occasionally. Taking a taxi instead of public transportation every once in a while won't spoil your brain, but if the pattern of taxi-taking becomes predictable, expect that your brain will no longer stand for the bus.

Best of all, to practice gratitude, create a ritual out of looking back on how far you've come. Cesar Kuriyama was so inspired to hold on to gratitude that he created an entire smartphone app just to capture his memories and look back on them later. It's called 1 Second Everyday and it allows users to collect snippets of their experiences every day. In an interview Cesar told us, "I think of my friends . . . I think how a couple of years ago they desperately wanted a job and a decent apartment, and now they have it, but it's not what they want anymore. Now they want all these other things, like a better job and a better apartment . . . and I bet once they get it, they'll want more again. Wouldn't it be nice if they sat down one day and reflected on how things were years ago? Realized they accomplished what they wanted back then . . . maybe celebrated . . . smiled . . . maybe realized that what they have now is actually enough . . . and be happier people for it." Psychologists agree. Researchers have found that counting our blessings regularly improves our well-being and heightens optimism.[9] Next time you experience a positive surprise, try this: stop and celebrate it. Feel thankful. Every night before going to bed, at mealtime, or every morning, get in the habit of readjusting your expectation bar. Think about the significance and the relative magnitude of all the wonderful things in your life. Name at least three pleasant surprises you experienced that day. Amazingly, the more we practice gratitude, the more life surprises us with reasons to be grateful.

THINK LIKE A SURPRISOLOGIST

Find just one way to surprise yourself every single day, whether it's through collecting novelty, turning on wonder, seeking awe, growing your comfort zone, or practicing gratitude. Schedule time on your calendar for surprise, use surprise as a tool whenever you are stuck or overwhelmed, or simplest of all: Remember to think like a Surprisologist. Asking, "What would a Surprisologist do?" is a shortcut to all the insights and ideas you've picked up in this book.

- I'm not sure if I should go out tonight. What would a Surprisologist do?
- How can I end this argument? What would a Surprisologist do?
- What should I say to keep everyone's attention? What would a Surprisologist do?
- How do I turn up the vibrancy in my life? You get the idea.

• • •

We're just about through, but before we go, we have a confession to make. This chapter hasn't only been about you. Yes, it's true that surprising yourself and thinking like a Surprisologist will make your life richer, but that's just one small victory. By embracing and engineering surprise you can make our whole *world* richer too. You can inspire wonder, connection, vulnerability, growth, and creativity. All you have to do is keep asking, What would a Surprisologist do?

THE BITE-SIZE VERSION

When we are surprised we feel deeply connected and thoroughly alive. Surprising ourselves every day is a vital part of living a happy life.

TOOLS

- **Collect novelty:** try new things, visit new places, and meet new people. Novelty stimulates dopamine, the neurochemical associated with interest and motivation.
- **Turn on wonder:** slow down and look at the world with fresh eyes. Seek out small surprises that you've never noticed. Say, "I wonder . . ." often and see what happens.
- **Seek awe:** surround yourself with experiences that make you feel like part of something larger (nature, intricate design, extraordinary skill, admirable moral acts). Awe slows down our perception of time and makes us more helpful.
- **Grow your comfort zone:** stretch across the imaginary line of your comfort zone every day. Keep in mind that as time passes, we regret the things we do not do.
- **Practice gratitude:** create rituals to periodically reset your expectation bars.

EXERCISE YOUR SURPRISE MUSCLE

Your final mission is to turn surprise into a habit. How will you remember to think like a Surprisologist? Choose an anchor that will become your reminder. For example, every time you hear the sound of a car horn or see a dime, check in to see whether you are surprising yourself regularly. What will your anchor be? What is one small way that you can surprise yourself today? Ask yourself, "What would a Surprisologist do?"

The End

No, really. We mean it this time.

··· SURPRISE FILE ···

Use this space to jot down your surprise ideas.

NAME

IDEAS & SURPRISE

OPPORTUNITIES

(fold here to keep)

TOP SECRET

··· **THANK YOU!** ···

From Tania and LeeAnn To:

Everyone who preread the book and jumped down the surprise rabbit hole with us:

Ashley Albert: who has the best ideas

Julie Jackson: who asks the best questions

Jason Forest: whose imagination makes life magical

Steve Nelson: who has the wisdom of a hundred-year-old and the whimsy of a ten-year-old

Thomas Wedell-Wedellsborg: who is an innovation and titulfication expert

Kevin Prentiss: who always gets it

Mariko Gordon: who lives gracefully in the unknown

Paloma Medina: who has witchy powers of insight

Cesar Kuriyama: who reminds us that moments matter

Joaquin Roca: who is the triple threat—brilliant, creative, and generous

Roi Ben-Yehuda: whose book on surprise we hope to read next

Raghava KK: who philosophizes like an artist and makes art like a philosopher

David Burk: who has taught us to think bigger

Jeff Wirth: who has taught us to think like experience designers

Hannah Kane: who is serious about fun and fun about serious

Becky Stella: who reminds us to stay true to our vision

Maya Gilbert: who has been there since the beginning

Our research assistants, Maria Guzman, Jonah Raskas, Leah Kashani, Bianca Rosa, Danny Mejia, Helen Lee, Ilmira Estil, and Roberly Aladin: your effort, wonder, and endless patience with data remind us that science is joyful when you work with wonderful people.

Katherine Fausset: who took a chance on us and stuck it out even when the road was paved with uncertainty. Who celebrated every victory and shrugged off setbacks. Whose email address we're classically conditioned to associate with exciting news. **And the Curtis Brown team:** who has held our hands through the ups, downs, and winding paths of this surprise journey.

Meg Leder: who has resuscitated our ideas by guiding us toward clarity. Who believes in surprise so much that she wears mismatched earrings and surprises her sales team. Who turned a lot of words into a book we love. **And the Perigee team:** who instantly won us over with its boldness, playfulness, and curiosity. We stand taller knowing that you are in our corner.

The clients and students of LifeLabs New York: for your bright minds, great ideas, and love of life's experiments.

To the clients, experience providers, and volunteers of Surprise Industries: for your courage, playfulness, and willingness to step into the unknown. Without you, we'd just be a bunch of weirdos.

From Tania to:

My students: who keep me on my toes and learning.

Mom: who laughs so hard it sounds like she's crying and who has always taken me seriously.

Grandma: who once made me a swing from a broken lawn chair and read me stories as I swung.

Kat: my partner in business, surprise, sisterhood, and making the impossible reality.

Leon: who believes in playfulness even when he looks dead serious (and is a true part of our family).

Carolyn: whose victory dances epitomize victory. Who teaches me to notice the little things.

Scarlett, Loki, and Spliooshka: who covered me in their fur and tenderness and filled the room with snorts and purrs and little dog and cat dreams as I wrote this book.

Brian: who may be a figment of my imagination because he's everything I've ever wanted. The certainty *and* surprise on my seesaw. I've never felt so safe. I've never had this much fun.

LeeAnn: who finds everything so interesting that it reminds you the world is a fascinating place. When we speak together, it's an adventure. When we teach together, I always learn something new. I can't remember a time we weren't writing together, and I can't wait for the next book.

From LeeAnn to:

Mom: for your unending kindness and heart as big as the ocean.

Dad: for being constantly curious, for teaching me so many of life's little lessons, and for never being afraid to be who you are.

My family: no matter how long it's been, it feels like home whenever I'm with you.

Ever: who is wild like a horse. And **Elle:** who once chased after the moon. You girls make me smile just thinking of your names.

Meg: for your playfulness and friendship over so many years. I'll never forget you coming across the parking lot and saying, "Whatcha up to?" You embrace surprise at its fullest.

Professors Marsha Green, Joel Wade, and Karl Grammer: for your wonder-filled classes.

Aaron, Rachel, Julius, Katharina, and Fritz (84 Engert Family): for so many delightful days.

Dirk: for being my lighthouse, rock, and oars. We've been down so many roads together. I feel so lucky to be by your side.

Tania: for inspiring me with every single conversation (and one more thing!). It has been such a great journey together. I look forward to the eighty delight-filled years ahead.

PART I. UNDERSTAND SURPRISE

1. James A. Russell, "Is There Universal Recognition of Emotion from Facial Expression? A Review of the Cross-Cultural Studies," *Psychological Bulletin* 115, no. 1 (1994): 102–141. doi: 10.1037/0033-2909.115.1.102. A review of research on the universality of emotions. Most studies have found that surprise is recognized in a wide range of cultures (most of all in Western countries).

2. Andrew Ortony and Terence J. Turner, "What's Basic About Basic Emotions?" *Psychological Review* 97, no. 3 (1990): 315–331. doi: 10.1037/0033-295X.97.3.315. See pages 317–318 for a good overview of the debate on whether surprise is an emotion.

CHAPTER 1. SURPRISE IN THE BRAIN

1. Rainer Reisenzein and Markus Studtmann, "On the Expression and Experience of Surprise: No Evidence for Facial Feedback, but Evidence for a Reverse Self-Interference Effect," *Emotion* 7 (2007): 612–627. doi: 10.1037/1528-3542.7.3.612.

2. Emanuel Donchin, "Surprise! . . . Surprise?" *Psychophysiology* 18, no. 5 (1981): 493–513. doi: 10.1111/j.1469-8986.1981.tb01815.x. Antonio Kolossa, Tim Fingscheidt, Karl Wessel, and Bruno Kopp, "A Model-Based Approach to Trial-by-Trial P300 Amplitude Fluctuations," *Frontiers in Human Neuroscience* 6, no. 359 (2013): 1–18. doi: 10.3389/Fnhum.2012.00359. Two reviews of the P300 (for those who really want to dig into the science of it).

3. Silvan S. Tomkins, *Affect, Imagery, Consciousness: The Positive Affects*, vol. 1 (New York: Springer Publishing, 1962).

4. In 2013, Tania Luna facilitated a Surprisology Studio for a group of students at NuVu Studio. They conducted an experiment together in which participants watched a video containing a surprise. They recorded participants' reactions to spot the Freeze and Find Phases of the Surprise Sequence.

5. Eva-Maria Gortner and James W. Pennebaker, "The Archival Anatomy of a Disaster: Media Coverage and Community-Wide Health Effects of the Texas A&M Bonfire Tragedy," *Journal of Social and Clinical Psychology* 22 (2003): 580–603. doi: 10.1521/jscp.22.5.580.22923. A fascinating examination of the consequences of disaster. For a less academic review, we highly recommend *The Secret Life of Pronouns* by James W. Pennebaker (New York: Bloomsbury Press, 2011).

6. Norbert Schwarz, *Stimmung als Information: Untersuchungen zum Einfluß von Stimmungen auf die Bewertung des eigenen Lebens* [Mood As Information: Investigations on the Influence of Moods] (Heidelberg, Germany: Springer Verlag, 1987). For an English account of how small surprises influence mood, see Chapter 4, edited by Daniel Kahneman, Ed Diener, and Norbert Schwarz, in the book *Well-Being: Foundations of Hedonic Psychology* (New York: Russell Sage Foundation, 2003).

7. Magnus Söderlund, "Customer Satisfaction and Its Consequences on Customer Behaviour Revisited: The Impact of Different Levels of Satisfaction on Word-of-Mouth, Feedback to Supplier and Loyalty," *International Journal of Service Industry Management* 9 (1998): 169–188. The term *cognitive burden* in the context of surprise seems to originate from this article.

8. Bernard Rimé, "Can Socially Sharing Emotions Change Emotions?" in *Changing Emotions*, edited by Dirk Hermans, Bernard Rimé, and Batja Mesquita (New York: Psychology Press, 2013), 91–96. Bernard Rimé, Batja Mesquita, Pierre Philippot, and Stefano Boca, "Beyond the Emotional Event: Six Studies on the Social Sharing of Emotions," *Cogni-*

tion et Emotion 5 (1991): 436–466. doi: 10.1080/02699939108411052. A terrific overview of the major studies and findings on emotion and social sharing.

9. Bernard Rimé, Pierre Philippot, Stefano Boca, and Batja Mesquita, "Long Lasting Cognitive and Social Consequences of Emotion: Social Sharing and Rumination," *European Review of Social Psychology* 3 (1992): 225–258 [edited by W. Stroebe and M. Hewstone]. See pages 248–252: The more surprising an event, the sooner and more we share it.

10. Catrin Finkenauer and Bernard Rimé, "Keeping Emotional Memories Secret: Health and Subjective Well-Being When Emotions Are Not Shared," *Journal of Health Psychology* 3, no. 1 (1998): 47–58. doi: 10.11 77/135910539800300104.

11. L. Michael Slepian, E. J. Masicampo, Negin R. Toosi, and Nalini Ambady, "The Physical Burdens of Secrecy," *Journal of Experimental Psychology: General* 141 (2012): 619–624. doi: 10.1037/a0027598.

12. Todd B. Kashdan and Michael F. Steger, "Curiosity and Pathways to Well-Being and Meaning in Life: Traits, States, and Everyday Behaviors," *Motivation and Emotion* 31 (2007): 159–183. doi: 10.1007/s11031 -007-9068-7. For a less academic account of curiosity, see the book *Curious? Discover the Missing Ingredient to a Fulfilling Life* (New York: HarperCollins, 2009). Kashdan is as infatuated with curiosity as we are with surprise!

13. Söderlund, "Customer Satisfaction and Its Consequences on Customer Behaviour Revisited."

14. "Professor Wolfram Schultz," Cambridge Neuroscience, University of Cambridge; www.neuroscience.cam.ac.uk/directory/profile.php ?Schultz. A directory of Schultz's extensive research on surprise, ambiguity, and more.

15. Dolf Zillmann, "Sequential Dependencies in Emotional Experience and Behavior," in *Emotion: Interdisciplinary Perspectives*, edited by R. D. Kavanaugh, B. Zimmerberg, and S. Fein (New Jersey: Lawrence Erlbaum Associates, 1996), 243–272. A good introduction to excitation-

transfer theory: when one emotion or experience "transfers" over into the next.

CHAPTER 2. SURPRISE IN THE WORLD

1. Judith Goldsmith, "Statistic," American Federation of Certified Psychics and Mediums Inc.; americanfederationofcertifiedpsychicsandmediums.org/statistics.htm.

2. Kiran Chetry, *American Morning*, CNN, February 6, 2009; transcripts .cnn.com/TRANSCRIPTS/0902/06/ltm.02.html. Includes an interview with Dr. Gita Johar.

3. Marion Martin, Gaynor Sadlo, and Graham Stew, "The Phenomenon of Boredom," *Qualitative Research in Psychology* 3 (2006): 193–211. doi: 10.1191/1478088706qrp066oa. An overview of boredom research (including what causes it and how to reduce it). Irene Tsapelas, Arthur Aron, and Terri Orbuch, "Marital Boredom Now Predicts Less Satisfaction 9 Years Later," *Psychological Science* 20, no. 5 (2009): 543–545. doi: 10.1111/j.1467-9280.2009.02332.x. Reinhard Pekrun, Nathan C. Hall, Thomas Goetz, and Raymond P. Perry, "Boredom and Academic Achievement: Testing a Model of Reciprocal Causation," *Journal of Educational Psychology* (2014): 1–15. doi: 10.1037/a0036006.

4. Alexander Marshack, *The Roots of Civilization: The Cognitive Beginning of Man's First Art, Symbol and Notation* (New York: McGraw-Hill, 1972).

5. Vernor Vinge, "What Is the Singularity?" paper presented at the VISION-21 Symposium, March 30–31, 1993; mindstalk.net/vinge/vinge-sing.html.

6. United Nations Cyberschoolbus, "Information and Communications Technology (ICT)"; un.org/cyberschoolbus/briefing/technology/tech .pdf.

7. Ray Kurzweil, "The Law of Accelerating Returns," Kurzweil Accelerating Intelligence, March 7, 2001; kurzweilai.net/the-law-of-accelerating -returns.

8. Vernor Vinge, "What Is the Singularity?"

9. Yue Wang, "More People Have Cell Phones Than Toilets, U.N. Study Shows," *Time*, March 25, 2013; newsfeed.time.com/2013/03/25/more-people-have-cell-phones-than-toilets-u-n-study-shows.

10. Jeanne Meister, "Job Hopping Is the 'New Normal' for Millennials: Three Ways to Prevent a Human Resource Nightmare," *Forbes*, August 14, 2012; forbes.com/sites/jeannemeister/2012/08/14/job-hopping-is-the-new-normal-for-millennials-three-ways-to-prevent-a-human-resource-nightmare. Note: The U.S. Bureau of Labor Statistics warns that it is difficult to determine whether job hopping is really on the rise because there have been no cross-generational longitudinal studies. While it seems that there is a trend toward changing jobs more frequently, this rate of change may slow down as the economy becomes more stable.

11. Steven P. Martin, "Delayed Marriage and Childbearing: Implications and Measurement of Diverging Trends in Family Timing," Department of Sociology and Maryland Population Research Center, October 2002; russellsage.org/sites/all/files/u4/Martin.pdf. Patricia Frank, "Rise of the Renter," *BedTimes*, March 2013; bedtimesmagazine.com/2013/03/rise-of-the-renter-what-changing-patterns-of-home ownership-mean-for-mattress-manufacturers.

12. YouTube, "Statistics: Viewership"; youtube.com/yt/press/statistics.html.

13. Ellen Weissinger, "Effects of Boredom on Self-Reported Health," *Society and Leisure* 18, no. 1 (1995): 21–32. doi: 10.1080/07053436.1995. 10715488. High boredom scores resulted in more self-reports of poor health (for more research on boredom see note 3 in this chapter).

PART II. EMBRACE THE UNPREDICTABLE

1. To learn more about the Emotion Regulation Lab, visit urban.hunter .cuny.edu/~tdennis/research.html. For more information about the Black Box experiment, see Ellen M. Kessel, Rebecca F. Huselid, Jennifer M. DeCicco, and Tracy A. Dennis, "Neurophysiological Processing of Emotion and Parenting Interact to Predict Inhibited Behavior: An Affective-Motivational Framework," *Frontiers in Human Neuroscience*

7 (2013): 1–14. doi: 10.3389/fnhum.2013.00326. In this study, children's reactions to the Black Box were correlated with parenting style and children's neural reactions to negative images. Kids whose brains reacted intensely to negative images were more hesitant to reach into the box, but only if their parents tended to focus on preventing harm and pointing out danger (rather than focusing on rewards).

CHAPTER 3. BUILD RESILIENCE

1. Christopher F. Sharpley and Pricilla Yardley, "The Relationship between Cognitive Hardiness, Explanatory Style and Depression-Happiness in Post-Retirement Men and Women," *Australian Psychologist* 34 (1999): 198–203. Suzanne C. Kobasa, "Stressful Life Events, Personality and Health: An Inquiry into Hardiness," *Journal of Personality and Social Psychology* 37 (1979): 1–11.

2. Eric Klinenberg, "Adaptation: How Can Cities Be 'Climate-Proofed'?" *New Yorker*, January 7, 2013; newyorker.com/reporting/2013/01/07/130107fa_fact_klinenberg.

3. Matthew K. Nock, "Actions Speak Louder Than Words: An Elaborated Theoretical Model of the Social Functions of Self-Injury and Other Harmful Behaviors," *Applied & Preventive Psychology* 12 (2008): 159–168. doi: 10.1016/j.appsy.2008.05.002.

4. Mihaly Csikszentmihalyi, *Creativity: Flow and the Psychology of Discovery and Invention* (New York: HarperCollins, 1996). We highly recommend this book. Not only is it a terrific overview of creative thinking but it also examines the role of routine and surprise in creativity.

5. "Five-on-Your-Side Is the Magic Number for a Personal Support Network," Nationwide, July 2012; nationwide.co.uk/about/media-centre-and-specialist-areas/media-centre/press-releases/archive/2012/7/five-on-your-side-is-the-magic-number-for-a-personal-support-network.

6. Tracy A. Dennis and Greg Hajcak, "The Late Positive Potential: A Neurophysiological Marker for Emotion Regulation in Children," *Journal of Child Psychology and Psychiatry* 50 (2009): 1373–1383. doi:

10.1111/j.1469-7610.2009.02168.x. A review of reappraisal (that is, re-framing) research and a study on reappraisal in children. All partici-pants except for girls aged five to six showed neural reappraisal after they heard a neutral story describing a negative image.

7. Pamela Weintraub, "The New Survivors," *Psychology Today*, July 2009; psychologytoday.com/articles/200906/the-new-survivors.

8. Karen Salmansohn, *The Bounce Back Book: How to Thrive in the Face of Adversity, Setbacks, and Losses* (New York: Workman, 2007).

9. Eva-Maria Gortner and James W. Pennebaker, "The Archival Anatomy of a Disaster: Media Coverage and Community-Wide Health Effects of the Texas A&M Bonfire Tragedy," *Journal of Social and Clinical Psychology* 22, no. 5 (2003): 580–603. doi: 10.1521/jscp.22.5.580.22923.

10. Lisa G. Aspinwall and Atara MacNamara, "Taking Positive Changes Seriously," *Cancer* 104 (2005): 2549–2556. doi: 10.1002/cncr.21244.

11. Richard G. Tedeschi and Lawrence G. Calhoun, "Posttraumatic Growth: Conceptual Foundations and Empirical Evidence," *Psychological Inquiry* 14, no. 1 (2004): 1–18. doi: 10.1207/s15327965pli1501_01.

12. Quoted in Weintraub, "The New Survivors."

CHAPTER 4. REFRAME VULNERABILITY

1. Karen Bartsch and David Estes, "Children's and Adults' Everyday Talk About Surprise," *British Journal of Developmental Psychology* 15 (2011): 461–475. doi: 10.1111/j.2044-835X.1997.tb00741.x.

2. Ethan Kross, Marc G. Berman, Walter Mischel, Edward E. Smith, and Tor D. Wager, "Social Rejection Shares Somatosensory Representations with Physical Pain," *Proceedings of the National Academy of Sciences* 108 (2010): 6270–6275. doi: 10.1073/pnas.1102693108.

3. C. S. Lewis, *The Four Loves* (New York: Houghton Mifflin Harcourt, 1960).

4. Daniel Ellsberg, "Risk, Ambiguity, and the Savage Axioms," *The Quarterly Journal of Economics* 75, no. 4 (1961): 643–669; jstor.org/stable/1884324.

5. Daniel Ellsberg, "Reply," *The Quarterly Journal of Economics* 77, no. 2

(1963): 336–342; jstor.org/stable/1884409. Uzi Segal, "The Ellsberg Paradox and Risk Aversion: An Anticipated Utility Approach," *International Economic Review* 28, no. 1 (1987): 175–202; jstor.org/stable/2526866.

6. Ming Hsu, Mehul Bhatt, Ralph Adolphs, Daniel Tranel, and Colin F. Camerer, "Neural Systems Responding to Degrees of Uncertainty in Human Decision-Making," *Science* 310, no. 5754 (2005): 1680–1883. doi: 10.1126/science.1115327.

7. Emma C. Winton, David M. Clark, and Robert J. Edelmann, "Social Anxiety, Fear of Negative Evaluation and the Detection of Negative Emotion in Others," *Behavior Research and Therapy* 33 (1995): 193–196. doi: 10.1016/0005-7967(94)E0019-F.

8. Stefan T. Trautmann, Ferdinand M. Vieider, and Peter P. Wakker, "Causes of Ambiguity Aversion: Known Versus Unknown Preferences," *Journal of Risk and Uncertainty* 36, no. 3 (2008): 225–243. doi: 10.1007/s11166-008-9038-9.

9. Elliot Aronson, Ben Willerman, and Joanne Floyd, "The Effect of a Pratfall on Increasing Interpersonal Attractiveness," *Psychonomic Science* 4, no. 6 (1996): 227–228. doi: 10.3758/BF03342263.

10. Brené Brown, *Expanding Perceptions*, TEDx video, 2010, http://youtu.be/X4Qm9cGRub0.

11. "April 2012 Trend Briefing: Flawsome," trendwatching.com, trendwatching.com/trends/flawsome.

12. Bernard Rimé, Pierre Philippot, Stefano Boca, and Batja Mesquita, "Long Lasting Cognitive and Social Consequences of Emotion: Social Sharing and Rumination," *European Review of Social Psychology* 3 (1992): 225–258 [edited by W. Stroebe and M. Hewstone]; see pages 234–238. See also Bernard Rimé, Batja Mesquita, Pierre Philippot, and Stefano Boca, "Beyond the Emotional Event: Six Studies on the Social Sharing of Emotions," *Cognition et Emotion* 5 (1991): 436–466.

13. LeeAnn Renninger, "A Darwinian Analysis of the Roles of Facial Attractiveness and Facial Expressiveness in Creating a First Impression," thesis, Faculty of Natural Sciences, University of Vienna, 2004.

14. James Baraz and Shoshana Alexander, "The Helper's High," Greater Good: The Science of a Meaningful Life, February 2001; greatergood .berkeley.edu/article/item/the_helpers_high.

CHAPTER 5. PRACTICE SKILLFUL NOT-KNOWING

1. Rolf Verleger, Piotr Jaskowski, and Bernd Wauschkuhn, "Suspense and Surprise: On the Relationship between Expectancies and P3," *Psychophysiology* 31 (1994): 359–369.
2. Timothy D. Wilson and Daniel T. Gilbert, "Explaining Away: A Model of Affective Adaptation," *Perspectives on Psychological Science* 3, no. 5 (2008): 370–386. doi: 10.1111/j.1745-6924.2008.00085.x.
3. Brendan Nyhan and Jason Reifler, "When Corrections Fail: The Persistence of Political Misperceptions," *Political Behavior* 32 (2010): 303–330. doi: 10.1007/s11109-010-9112-2.
4. Stephen S. Hall, *Wisdom: From Philosophy to Neuroscience* (New York: Vintage Books, 2011), 48–53.
5. Paul Saffo, "Strong Opinions Weakly Held," *Paul Saffo* [blog], July 26, 2008; saffo.com/02008/07/26/strong-opinions-weakly-held.
6. Adrian Furnham and Joseph Marks. "Tolerance of Ambiguity: A Review of the Recent Literature," *Psychology* 4, no. 9 (2013): 717–728. doi: dx.doi.org/10.4236/psych.2013.49102.
7. Paul West and David Lauter, "On Gay Marriage, Change in Public Opinion Has Been Big, and Rapid," *Los Angeles Times,* March 26, 2013; articles.latimes.com/2013/mar/26/news/la-pn-gay-marriage -public-opinion-20130326.

CHAPTER 6. GET CREATIVE

1. Joe Sharkey, "Reinventing the Suitcase by Adding the Wheel," *New York Times*, October 4, 2010; nytimes.com/2010/10/05/business/05road .html.
2. "History Timeline: Post-it Note Notes," Post-it; post-it.com/wps/ portal/3M/en_US/PostItNA/Home/Support/About.
3. D. O. Hebb, *The Organization of Behavior: A Neuropsychological Theory*

(New York: Wiley, 1949). Donald introduces the idea that neurons that fire together, wire together. He proposes that our brains form "cell-assemblies" or networks of associated ideas. Only once we have these cell-assemblies can we rearrange them to form new insights and ideas.

4. "Shinkansen Train," AskNature; asknature.org/product/6273d963ef015 b98f641fc2b67992a5e#menuPopup.

5. Mary Oppezzo and Daniel L. Schwartz, "Give Your Idea Legs: The Positive Effect of Walking on Creative Thinking," *Journal of Experimental Psychology: Learning, Memory, and Cognition* 40, no. 4 (2014): 1142–1152. doi: 10.1037/a0036577.

6. Hayagreeva Rao, Robert Sutton, and Allen P. Webb, "Innovation Lessons from Pixar: An Interview with Oscar-Winning Director Brad Bird," *McKinsey Quarterly*, April 2008; mckinsey.com/insights/innovation/innovation_lessons_from_pixar_an_interview_with_oscar-winning_director_brad_bird.

7. "Darryl F. Zanuck: Biography," IMDb; imdb.com/name/nm0953123/bio.

CHAPTER 7. WIELD ATTENTION

1. Corey Kilgannon, "Dancing with Cars," *New York Times*, November 1, 2013; nytimes.com/2013/11/03/nyregion/dancing-with-the-cars.html.

2. Thomas H. Davenport and John C. Beck, *The Attention Economy: Understanding the New Currency of Business* (Boston: Harvard Business Review Press, 2002).

3. "Changing Channels: Americans View Just 17 Channels Despite Record Number to Choose From" [newswire], Nielsen, May 6, 2014; nielsen.com/us/en/newswire/2014/changing-channels-americans-view-just-17-channels-despite-record-number-to-choose-from.html.

4. "Online Dating Statistics," Statistic Brain, January 1, 2014; statisticbrain.com/online-dating-statistics.

5. Boguslaw Zernicki, "Pavlovian Orienting Reflect," *Acta Neurobiology Experimentalis* 47 (1927): 239–247; ane.pl/pdf/4721.pdf. A review of

Ivan Pavlov's theory. It turns out Pavlov was something of a Surprisologist too!

6. Jakob Nielsen, "How Long Do Users Stay on Web Pages?" Nielsen Norman Group, September 12, 2011; nngroup.com/articles/how-long-do-users-stay-on-web-pages.

7. Rob Weatherhead, "Say It Quick, Say It Well: The Attention Span of a Modern Internet Consumer," *Media Network* [blog], February 28, 2014; theguardian.com/media-network/media-network-blog/2012/mar/19/attention-span-internet-consumer.

8. Jon Van, "Natural Selection: Rather Than Their Brains, TV Channel Surfers May Simply Be Proving Darwin's Theory," *Chicago Tribune*, November 3, 1995, articles.chicagotribune.com/1995-11-03/features/9511030164_1_channel-surfing-attention-span-attention-deficit-disorder/2.

9. Virginia Heffernan, "The Attention-Span Myth," *New York Times*, November 19, 2010; nytimes.com/2010/11/21/magazine/21FOB-medium-t.html?_r=1&.

10. Martin Guhn, Alfons Hamm, and Marcel Zentner, "Physiological and Musico-Acoustic Correlates of the Chill Response," *Music Perception: An Interdisciplinary Journal* 24, no. 5 (2007): 473–484. doi: 10.1525/mp.2007.24.5.473.

11. "Piano Staircase," The Fun Theory, September 22, 2009.

12. Seth Godin, "I'm Not Surprised," Seth's Blog [blog], February 24, 2007; sethgodin.typepad.com/seths_blog/2007/02/im_not_surprise.html.

13. J. J. Abrams, *The Mystery Box*, TED video, March 2007; ted.com/talks/j_j_abrams_mystery_box.

14. Andrew Stanton, *The Clues to a Great Story*, TED video, 2012; ted.com/talks/andrew_stanton_the_clues_to_a_great_story.

15. David Johnson, "The Element of Surprise an Effective Classroom Technique," *The Mathematics Teacher* 66 (1973): 13–16; jstor.org/stable/27959162.

CHAPTER 8. DESIGN DELIGHT

1. Warren D. Houten, *A General Theory of Emotions and Social Life* (New York: Routledge, 2006), 77–78.

2. John C. Crotts and Vince Magnini, "The Customer Delight Construct: Is Surprise Essential?" *Annals of Tourism Research* 37, no. 4 (2011): 719–722. doi: 10.1016/j.annals.2010.03.004.

3. Bernard Rimé, Batja Mesquita, Pierre Philippot, and Stefano Boca, "Beyond the Emotional Event: Six Studies on the Social Sharing of Emotions," *Cognition et Emotion* 5 (1991): 436–466. doi: 10.1080/02699939108411052.

4. Karuna Subramaniam, John Kounios, Todd B. Parrish, and Mark Jung-Beeman, "A Brain Mechanism for Facilitation of Insight by Positive Affect," *Journal of Cognitive Neuroscience* 21, no. 3 (2009): 415–432. doi: 10.1162/jocn.2009.21057.

5. Wolfram Schultz, Paul Apicella, and Tomas Ljungberg, "Responses of Monkey Dopamine Neurons to Reward and Conditioned Stimuli During Successive Steps of Learning a Delayed Response Task," *Journal of Neuroscience* 13, no. 3 (1993): 900–913. jneurosci.org/content/13/3/900.long.

6. Kent C. Berridge, "The Debate over Dopamine's Role in Reward: The Case for Incentive Salience," *Psychopharmacology* 191 (2007): 391–431. doi: 10.1007/s00213-006-0578-x.

7. Randy Garner, "Post-It Note Persuasion: A Sticky Influence," *Journal of Consumer Psychology* 15, no. 3 (2005): 230–237; media.cbsm.com/uploads/1/PostitNotePersuasion.pdf.

8. Ana Valenzuela, Barbara Mellers, and Judi Strebel, "Pleasurable Surprises: A Cross-Cultural Study of Consumer Responses to Unexpected Incentives," *Journal of Consumer Research* 36 (2010): 792–805. doi: 10.1086/605592.

9. Timothy D. Wilson, David B. Centerbar, and Deborah A. Kermer, "The Pleasures of Uncertainty: Prolonging Positive Moods in Ways People Do Not Anticipate," *Attitudes and Social Cognition* 88, no. 1 (2005): 5–21. doi: 10.1037/0022-3514.88.1.5.

CHAPTER 9. MAKE EXPERIENCES

1. B. Joseph Pine II and James H. Gilmore, "Welcome to the Experience Economy," *Harvard Business Review* 76 (1998): 97–105. hbr .org/1998/07/welcome-to-the-experience-economy.

2. Elizabeth W. Dunn, Daniel T. Gilbert, and Timothy D. Wilson, "If Money Doesn't Make You Happy, Then You Probably Aren't Spending It Right," *Journal of Consumer Psychology* 21, no. 2 (2011): 115–125. doi: 10.1016/j.jcps.2011.02.002.

3. Stephanie Rosenbloom, "But Will It Make You Happy?" *New York Times*, August 7, 2010; nytimes.com/2010/08/08/business/08consume .html?pagewanted=all.

4. "Transumers," Trendwatching, last modified November 2006; trend watching.com/trends/TRANSUMERS.htm.

5. U.S. Bureau of Labor Statistics, "Customer Expenditures in 2012," March 2014; bls.gov/cex/csxann12.pdf.

6. Daniel Pink, *A Whole New Mind* (New York: Riverhead, 2006).

7. Doris G. Bazzini, Elizabeth R. Stack, Penny D. Martincin, and Carmen P. Davis, "The Effect of Reminiscing About Laughter on Relationship Satisfaction," *Motivation and Emotion* 31, no. 1 (2007): 25–34. doi: 10.1007/s11031-006-9045-6.

8. B. Joseph Pine II and James H. Gilmore, *The Experience Economy* (Boston: Harvard Business Review Press, 2011), 107.

9. "Burning Man Timeline," Burning Man; burningman.com/whatis burningman/about_burningman/bm_timeline.html.

CHAPTER 10. CULTIVATE RELATIONSHIPS

1. Ken Mammarella, "Crossroads: Best Friends for 80 Years," *(Delaware) News Journal*, May 22, 2014; delawareonline.com/story/life/2014/05/21/ crossroads-best-friends-forever/9391447.

2. Peter Coleman, *The Five Percent: Finding Solutions to Seemingly Impossible Conflicts* (New York: Public Affairs, 2011).

3. Helen Fisher, *Why We Love: The Nature and Chemistry of Romantic Love* (New York: Henry Holt, 2004), 91–92.

4. Esther Perel, *The Secret to Desire in a Long-Term Relationship*, TED video, 2013; ted.com/talks/esther_perel_the_secret_to_desire_in_a_long_term_relationship.

5. Ibid.

6. James Patrick Kelly, "When Friends Get Together, Good Food Happens," *Idaho Statesman*, May 31, 2014; idahostatesman.com/2014/05/31/3208627/when-friends-get-together-good.html?sp=/99/109.

7. Arthur Aron, Christina C. Norman, Elaine N. Aron, Colin McKenna, and Richard E. Heyman, "Couples' Shared Participation in Novel and Arousing Activities and Experienced Relationship Quality," *Journal of Personality and Social Psychology* 78, no. 2 (2000): 273–284. doi: 10.1037/0022-3514.78.2.273.

8. "Research FAQs," Gottman Institute; gottman.com/research/research-faqs.

9. John M. Gottman, *Why Marriages Succeed or Fail* (New York: Fireside, 1994), p. 57.

10. Gary Chapman, *The 5 Love Languages: The Secret to Love That Lasts* (Chicago: Northfield Publishing, 2009).

11. Michele Weiner-Davis, *Divorce Busting* (New York: Fireside, 1992). We recommend this book to everyone (even if you are not married and don't plan to be).

CHAPTER 11. SURPRISE YOURSELF

1. Nico Bunzeck and Emrah E. Duzel, "Absolute Coding of Stimulus Novelty in the Human Substantia Nigra/VTA," *Neuron* 51, no 3 (2006): 369–379.

2. Jurgis Baltrusaitis and Richard Miller, *Aberrations: An Essay on the Legend of Forms* (Cambridge, MA: MIT Press, 1989), 61.

3. Todd B. Kashdan, *Curious? Discover the Missing Ingredient to a Fulfilling Life* (New York: HarperCollins, 2010).

4. Yoaz Bar-Anan, Timothy Wilson, and Dan Gilbert, "The Feeling of Uncertainty Intensifies Affective Reactions," *Emotion* 9, no. 1 (2009): 123–127. doi: 10.1037/a0014607123.

5. Melanie Rudd, Kathleen D. Vohs, and Jennifer Aaker, "Awe Expands People's Perception of Time, Alters Decision Making, and Enhances Well-Being," *Psychological Science* 23, no. 10 (2012): 1130–1136. doi: 10.1177/0956797612438731.

6. James Baraz and Shoshana Alexander, "The Helper's High." Greater Good, February 1, 2001; greatergood.berkeley.edu/article/item/the_helpers_high.

7. Thomas Gilovich and Victoria Husted Medvec, "The Experience of Regret: What, When, and Why," *Psychological Review* 102, no. 2 (1995): 379–395. doi: 10.1037/0033-295X.102.2.379.

8. Christopher Peterson, Willibald Ruch, Ursula Beermann, Nansook Park, and Martin E. P. Seligman, "Strengths of Character, Orientations to Happiness, and Life Satisfaction," *Journal of Positive Psychology* 2, no. 3 (2007): 149–156. doi: 10.1080/17439760701228938.

9. Robert A. Emmons and Michael E. McCullough, "Counting Blessings Versus Burdens: An Experimental Investigation of Gratitude and Subjective Well-Being in Daily Life," *Journal of Personality and Social Psychology* 84, no. 2 (2003): 377–389. doi: 10.1037/0022-3514.84.2.377.

Page numbers in *italics* indicate illustrations.

understimulation stress (hypostress), world (surprise in the), 22, 23–24, 31, 32–33
unexpected. *See* engineering the unexpected
unfolding mystery, attention (wielding), 127, 130–32, 133
Unifying Theory of 2+2, attention (wielding), 132
United Kingdom, xix
United Nations, 26
University of Vienna, xix, 117–18, 123, 131, 132
University of Virginia, 147
unknowns. *See* not-knowing, practicing skillful
unpredictable. *See* embracing the unpredictable
Upright Citizens Brigade, 88
urban legends, 13

varying delights, delights (designing), 149
Vinge, Vernor, 25, 26
Volkswagen's Fun Theory challenge, 125
vulnerability, reframing, 18, 41, 63–78, 99
    asking for help, 72, 76–77, 78
    certain vs. uncertain, 68–69, 69
    Cheat Sheet, 78
    closed vs. open, 68–69, 69
    coolness, enemy of growth, 66, 78
    distance, enemy of influence, 68–69, 78
    Ellsberg paradox, 67–70, 70
    exercising your surprise muscle, 78
    inviting vulnerability, 69–77, 70, 80
    mistakes, owning your, 72–74, 78
    next notching, 72, 74–76, 78
    openness = vulnerability, 65–69, 69, 78
    owning your mistakes, 72–74, 78
    protection, enemy of connection, 67–68, 78
    schemata, 65–66
    trait inventory, 68–69, 69
    weakness = vulnerability, 64–65, 78
    See also embracing the unpredictable
vulnerability (feeling on the spot), brain (surprise in the), 15–18

WALL-E (movie), 131
weakness = vulnerability, 64–65, 78
weather forecasts, 33, 34
wedding planners, 33
Wedell-Wedellsborg, Thomas, 105, 106, 114
Weinberg, Nick, 130
Weiner-Davis, Michele, 188

what-ifs, vulnerability (reframing), 65
"What is it?" (orienting response), 121
Whole New Mind, A (Pink), 157
wielding attention. *See* attention, wielding
Wilson, Timothy, 156, 196
wonder (turning on), yourself (surprising), 192, 194–96, *195*, 202, 204
words of affirmation (love language), relationships (cultivating), 184, 190
world, surprise in the, xxii, 18, 21–36
    adapting to a new ecosystem, 35, 36
    anxiety, 21, 23, 30, 31, 32, 36, 82–83
    boredom epidemic, 22, 23–24, 29–33, 36
    Cheat Sheet, 36
    control withdrawal, 29, 33–35
    exponential rate of change, 25–27, 36, 105
    Find Phase (Surprise Sequence Part Two), 23
    hypostress (stress of understimulation), 22, 23–24, 31, 32–33
    less surprising future, 28–35, 36
    more surprising future, 24–28, 34, 35, 36
    schemata, 34
    Surprise Seesaw, 22, 22–24, 31, 34, 35, 36
    See also Surprise Seesaw; understanding surprise
Wurman, Josh, 34

you -er (emotional intensification), brain (surprise in the), 15–17
yourself, surprising, 170, 191–204
    Cheat Sheet, 204
    collecting novelty, 192, 193–94, 202, 204
    exercising your surprise muscle, 204
    Find Phase (Surprise Sequence Part Two), 193, 194
    growing comfort zone, 192, 197–200, 202, 204
    practicing gratitude, 192, 200–202, 204
    seeking awe, 192, 196–97, 202, 204
    Shift Phase (Surprise Sequence Part Three), 193, 197
    thinking like a Surprisologist, 202–3, 204
    turning on wonder, 192, 194–96, *195*, 202, 204
    See also everyday surprise
YouTube, 13, 29, 105, 120–21, 145

Zanuck, Darryl, 114
Zappos, 68, 75–76

Tania Luna leads the culture department at LifeLabs New York, a company that helps people, teams, and organizations master life's most useful skills (from how to ask better questions to how to think more strategically). She is also the cofounder of Surprise Industries, the world's only company specializing in surprise. Tania writes for *Psychology Today* and conducts research on surprise.

LeeAnn Renninger, PhD, is the CEO and founder of LifeLabs New York. She received her PhD in social psychology from the University of Vienna, where she studied the differences between good and great communicators. At LifeLabs New York, she helps managers around the globe catalyze better (and more surprising) thinking in themselves and others.

Tania and LeeAnn have spoken at a wide range of corporate events and to TED, TEDx, Yahoo! Ignite, and YPO audiences. The authors provide training, organizational consulting, and team building for some of the world's most inspiring organizations, including Etsy, Whole Foods Market, Google, National Geographic, LinkedIn, Victoria's Secret, Warby Parker, Squarespace, Columbia University, and Yale University. Both authors live, work, and play in New York.

To learn more about Surprise Industries, visit SurpriseIndustries.com.

To learn more about LifeLabs New York, visit LifeLabsNewYork.com.

To contact the authors, email hey@surprisology.com.

For a surprise, call (646) 450-7475.

Jason Forest is the principal artist and founder of GreySoul Studio. He and fellow GreySoul creative Bruce Seaton write, design, and print Read-to-Me Comics. Jason uses digital media to enhance his painstakingly intricate pen-and-ink hand drawings, resulting in images that balance the visceral feel of traditional art with the slickness of digital design. When Jason isn't drawing pictures, he and his wife, Amanda, are professional knucklehead-herders, pulling splinters, repairing action figures, mending boo-boos, and hiking with their three sons.

For information on current and upcoming GreySoul projects, visit greysoulstudio.com.